Endpoint Protection Solutions
Complete Self-Assessment Guide

The guidance in this Self-Assessment is based on Endpoint Protection Solutions best practices and standards in business process architecture, design and quality management. The guidance is also based on the professional judgment of the individual collaborators listed in the Acknowledgments.

Notice of rights

You are licensed to use the Self-Assessment contents in your presentations and materials for internal use and customers without asking us - we are here to help.

Trademarks

Many of the designations used by manufacturers and sellers to distinguish their products are claimed as trademarks. Where those designations appear in this book, and the publisher was aware of a trademark claim, the designations appear as requested by the owner of the trademark. All other product names and services identified throughout this book are used in editorial fashion only and for the benefit of such companies with no intention of infringement of the trademark. No such use, or the use of any trade name, is intended to convey endorsement or other affiliation with this book.

Table of Contents

About The Art of Service

The Art of Service, Business Process Architects since 2000, is dedicated to helping stakeholders achieve excellence.

Defining, designing, creating, and implementing a process to solve a stakeholders challenge or meet an objective is the most valuable role... In EVERY group, company, organization and department.

Unless you're talking a one-time, single-use project, there should be a process. Whether that process is managed and implemented by humans, AI, or a combination of the two, it needs to be designed by someone with a complex enough perspective to ask the right questions.

Someone capable of asking the right questions and step back and say, 'What are we really trying to accomplish here? And is there a different way to look at it?'

With The Art of Service's Standard Requirements Self-Assessments, we empower people who can do just that — whether their title is marketer, entrepreneur, manager, salesperson, consultant, Business Process Manager, executive assistant, IT Manager, CIO etc... —they are the people who rule the future. They are people who watch the process as it happens, and ask the right questions to make the process work better.

Contact us when you need any support with this Self-Assessment and any help with templates, blue-prints and examples of standard documents you might need:

http://theartofservice.com
service@theartofservice.com

Included Resources - how to access

Included with your purchase of the book is the Endpoint

Protection Solutions Self-Assessment Spreadsheet Dashboard which contains all questions and Self-Assessment areas and auto-generates insights, graphs, and project RACI planning - all with examples to get you started right away.

How? Simply send an email to
access@theartofservice.com
with this books' title in the subject to get the Endpoint Protection Solutions Self Assessment Tool right away.

You will receive the following contents with New and Updated specific criteria:

- The latest quick edition of the book in PDF

- The latest complete edition of the book in PDF, which criteria correspond to the criteria in...

- The Self-Assessment Excel Dashboard, and...

- Example pre-filled Self-Assessment Excel Dashboard to get familiar with results generation

- In-depth specific Checklists covering the topic

- Project management checklists and templates to assist with implementation

INCLUDES LIFETIME SELF ASSESSMENT UPDATES

Every self assessment comes with Lifetime Updates and Lifetime Free Updated Books. Lifetime Updates is an industry-first feature which allows you to receive verified self assessment updates, ensuring you always have the most accurate information at your fingertips.

Get it now- you will be glad you did - do it now, before you forget.

Send an email to **access@theartofservice.com** with this books' title in the subject to get the Endpoint Protection Solutions Self Assessment Tool right away.

Purpose of this Self-Assessment

This Self-Assessment has been developed to improve understanding of the requirements and elements of Endpoint Protection Solutions, based on best practices and standards in business process architecture, design and quality management.

It is designed to allow for a rapid Self-Assessment to determine how closely existing management practices and procedures correspond to the elements of the Self-Assessment.

The criteria of requirements and elements of Endpoint Protection Solutions have been rephrased in the format of a Self-Assessment questionnaire, with a seven-criterion scoring system, as explained in this document.

In this format, even with limited background knowledge of Endpoint Protection Solutions, a manager can quickly review existing operations to determine how they measure up to the standards. This in turn can serve as the starting point of a 'gap analysis' to identify management tools or system elements that might usefully be implemented in the organization to help improve overall performance.

How to use the Self-Assessment

On the following pages are a series of questions to identify to what extent your Endpoint Protection Solutions initiative is complete in comparison to the requirements set in standards.

To facilitate answering the questions, there is a space in front of each question to enter a score on a scale of '1' to '5'.

1 Strongly Disagree

2 Disagree

3 Neutral

4 Agree

5 Strongly Agree

Read the question and rate it with the following in front of mind:

'In my belief,
the answer to this question is clearly defined'.

There are two ways in which you can choose to interpret this statement;
1. how aware are you that the answer to the question is clearly defined
2. for more in-depth analysis you can choose to gather evidence and confirm the answer to the question. This obviously will take more time, most Self-Assessment users opt for the first way to interpret the question and dig deeper later on based on the outcome of the overall Self-Assessment.

A score of '1' would mean that the answer is not clear at all, where a '5' would mean the answer is crystal clear and defined. Leave emtpy when the question is not applicable or you don't want to answer it, you can skip it without affecting your score. Write your score in the space provided.

After you have responded to all the appropriate statements in each section, compute your average score for that section, using the formula provided, and round to the nearest tenth. Then transfer to the corresponding spoke in the Endpoint Protection Solutions Scorecard on the second next page of the Self-Assessment.

Your completed Endpoint Protection Solutions Scorecard will give you a clear presentation of which Endpoint Protection Solutions areas need attention.

Endpoint Protection Solutions Scorecard Example

Example of how the finalized Scorecard can look like:

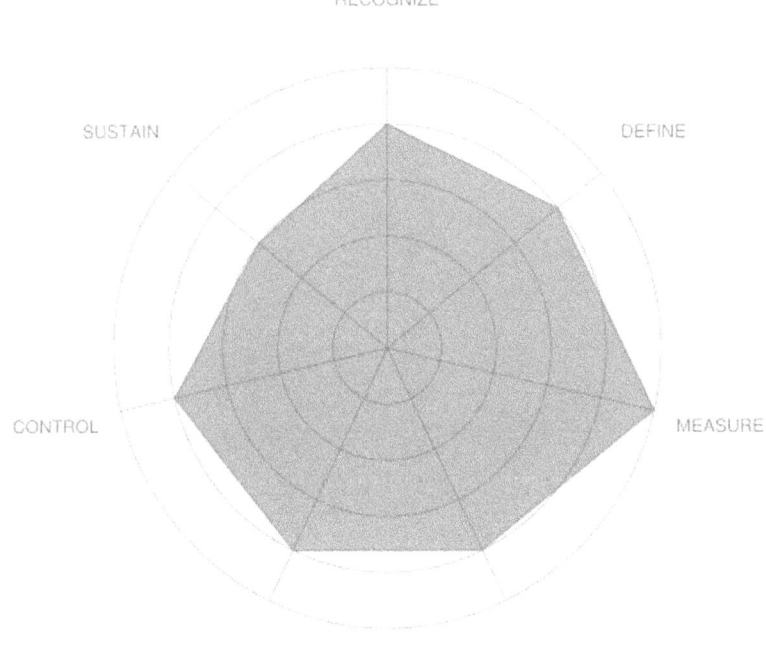

Endpoint Protection Solutions Scorecard

Your Scores:

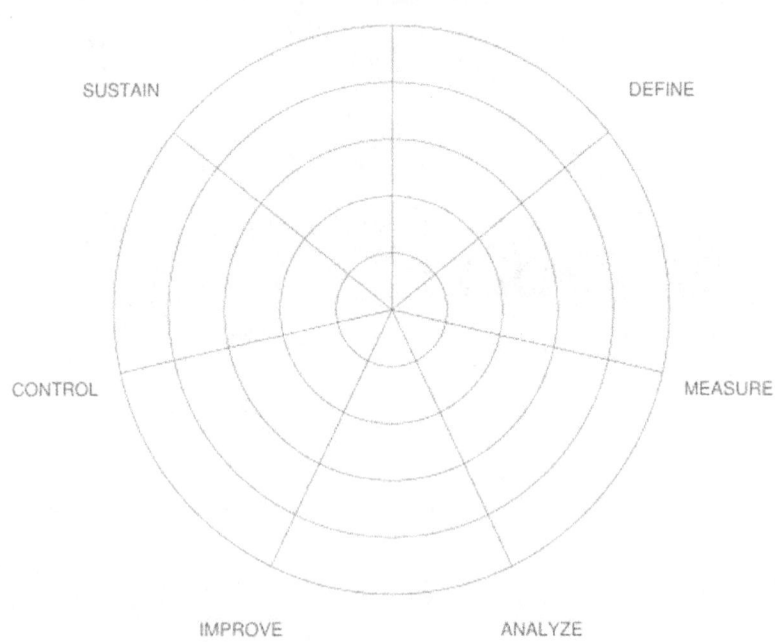

BEGINNING OF THE SELF-ASSESSMENT:

CRITERION #1: RECOGNIZE

INTENT: Be aware of the need for change. Recognize that there is an unfavorable variation, problem or symptom.

In my belief, the answer to this question is clearly defined:

5 Strongly Agree

4 Agree

3 Neutral

2 Disagree

1 Strongly Disagree

1. What endpoint protection solutions events should you attend?
<--- Score

2. What are the endpoint protection solutions resources needed?
<--- Score

3. Which needs are not included or involved?

<--- Score

4. Think about the people you identified for your endpoint protection solutions project and the project responsibilities you would assign to them, what kind of training do you think they would need to perform these responsibilities effectively?
<--- Score

5. How do you identify subcontractor relationships?
<--- Score

6. What are the timeframes required to resolve each of the issues/problems?
<--- Score

7. What endpoint protection solutions capabilities do you need?
<--- Score

8. What does endpoint protection solutions success mean to the stakeholders?
<--- Score

9. Will new equipment/products be required to facilitate endpoint protection solutions delivery, for example is new software needed?
<--- Score

10. For your endpoint protection solutions project, identify and describe the business environment, is there more than one layer to the business environment?
<--- Score

11. What do you need to start doing?

<--- Score

12. What should be considered when identifying available resources, constraints, and deadlines?
<--- Score

13. What do employees need in the short term?
<--- Score

14. Are there recognized endpoint protection solutions problems?
<--- Score

15. Do you know what you need to know about endpoint protection solutions?
<--- Score

16. How do you recognize an objection?
<--- Score

17. What endpoint protection solutions coordination do you need?
<--- Score

18. To what extent would your organization benefit from being recognized as a award recipient?
<--- Score

19. What resources or support might you need?
<--- Score

20. What activities does the governance board need to consider?
<--- Score

21. Are there endpoint protection solutions problems

defined?
<--- Score

22. How are you going to measure success?
<--- Score

23. What are the clients issues and concerns?
<--- Score

24. What creative shifts do you need to take?
<--- Score

25. Does your organization need more endpoint protection solutions education?
<--- Score

26. Is it clear when you think of the day ahead of you what activities and tasks you need to complete?
<--- Score

27. Looking at each person individually – does every one have the qualities which are needed to work in this group?
<--- Score

28. Who needs budgets?
<--- Score

29. What are the stakeholder objectives to be achieved with endpoint protection solutions?
<--- Score

30. What training and capacity building actions are needed to implement proposed reforms?
<--- Score

31. Will it solve real problems?
<--- Score

32. What extra resources will you need?
<--- Score

33. Where is training needed?
<--- Score

34. What endpoint protection solutions problem should be solved?
<--- Score

35. How do you recognize an endpoint protection solutions objection?
<--- Score

36. What is the extent or complexity of the endpoint protection solutions problem?
<--- Score

37. Is it needed?
<--- Score

38. Will a response program recognize when a crisis occurs and provide some level of response?
<--- Score

39. Consider your own endpoint protection solutions project, what types of organizational problems do you think might be causing or affecting your problem, based on the work done so far?
<--- Score

40. How are training requirements identified?
<--- Score

41. How many trainings, in total, are needed?
<--- Score

42. How much are sponsors, customers, partners, stakeholders involved in endpoint protection solutions? In other words, what are the risks, if endpoint protection solutions does not deliver successfully?
<--- Score

43. Is the need for organizational change recognized?
<--- Score

44. Did you miss any major endpoint protection solutions issues?
<--- Score

45. What information do users need?
<--- Score

46. Why is this needed?
<--- Score

47. To what extent does each concerned units management team recognize endpoint protection solutions as an effective investment?
<--- Score

48. Who should resolve the endpoint protection solutions issues?
<--- Score

49. What tools and technologies are needed for a custom endpoint protection solutions project?

<--- Score

50. Are you dealing with any of the same issues today as yesterday? What can you do about this?
<--- Score

51. Are there any specific expectations or concerns about the endpoint protection solutions team, endpoint protection solutions itself?
<--- Score

52. Who needs to know about endpoint protection solutions?
<--- Score

53. What is the endpoint protection solutions problem definition? What do you need to resolve?
<--- Score

54. Do you need to avoid or amend any endpoint protection solutions activities?
<--- Score

55. Does endpoint protection solutions create potential expectations in other areas that need to be recognized and considered?
<--- Score

56. What vendors make products that address the endpoint protection solutions needs?
<--- Score

57. How do you assess your endpoint protection solutions workforce capability and capacity needs, including skills, competencies, and staffing levels?
<--- Score

58. Are losses recognized in a timely manner?
<--- Score

59. Does the problem have ethical dimensions?
<--- Score

60. What else needs to be measured?
<--- Score

61. Who needs what information?
<--- Score

62. What is the smallest subset of the problem you can usefully solve?
<--- Score

63. How do you identify the kinds of information that you will need?
<--- Score

64. What are your needs in relation to endpoint protection solutions skills, labor, equipment, and markets?
<--- Score

65. Are your goals realistic? Do you need to redefine your problem? Perhaps the problem has changed or maybe you have reached your goal and need to set a new one?
<--- Score

66. How do you take a forward-looking perspective in identifying endpoint protection solutions research related to market response and models?
<--- Score

67. Are problem definition and motivation clearly presented?
<--- Score

68. Will endpoint protection solutions deliverables need to be tested and, if so, by whom?
<--- Score

69. Are there any revenue recognition issues?
<--- Score

70. Whom do you really need or want to serve?
<--- Score

71. Where do you need to exercise leadership?
<--- Score

72. What needs to be done?
<--- Score

73. How does it fit into your organizational needs and tasks?
<--- Score

74. What would happen if endpoint protection solutions weren't done?
<--- Score

75. Have you identified your endpoint protection solutions key performance indicators?
<--- Score

76. Are employees recognized or rewarded for performance that demonstrates the highest levels of integrity?

<--- Score

77. Who needs to know?
<--- Score

78. What are the expected benefits of endpoint protection solutions to the stakeholder?
<--- Score

79. As a sponsor, customer or management, how important is it to meet goals, objectives?
<--- Score

80. Are controls defined to recognize and contain problems?
<--- Score

81. What is the problem and/or vulnerability?
<--- Score

82. Is the quality assurance team identified?
<--- Score

83. Do you have/need 24-hour access to key personnel?
<--- Score

84. What is the recognized need?
<--- Score

85. Who else hopes to benefit from it?
<--- Score

86. Why the need?
<--- Score

87. Are there regulatory / compliance issues?
<--- Score

88. Which issues are too important to ignore?
<--- Score

**89. What prevents you from making the changes
you know will make you a more effective endpoint
protection solutions leader?**
<--- Score

90. Who are your key stakeholders who need to sign
off?
<--- Score

91. How are the endpoint protection solutions's
objectives aligned to the group's overall stakeholder
strategy?
<--- Score

92. Do you need different information or graphics?
<--- Score

93. Do you recognize endpoint protection solutions
achievements?
<--- Score

94. What problems are you facing and how do
you consider endpoint protection solutions will
circumvent those obstacles?
<--- Score

95. Which information does the endpoint protection
solutions business case need to include?
<--- Score

96. How can auditing be a preventative security measure?
<--- Score

97. When a endpoint protection solutions manager recognizes a problem, what options are available?
<--- Score

98. What are the minority interests and what amount of minority interests can be recognized?
<--- Score

99. What situation(s) led to this endpoint protection solutions Self Assessment?
<--- Score

Add up total points for this section:
_ _ _ _ _ = Total points for this section

Divided by: _ _ _ _ _ _ (number of statements answered) = _ _ _ _ _ _
Average score for this section

Transfer your score to the endpoint protection solutions Index at the beginning of the Self-Assessment.

CRITERION #2: DEFINE:

INTENT: Formulate the stakeholder problem. Define the problem, needs and objectives.

In my belief, the answer to this question is clearly defined:

5 Strongly Agree

4 Agree

3 Neutral

2 Disagree

1 Strongly Disagree

1. How have you defined all endpoint protection solutions requirements first?
<--- Score

2. What are the dynamics of the communication plan?
<--- Score

3. What are the endpoint protection solutions tasks and definitions?

<--- Score

4. Is endpoint protection solutions linked to key stakeholder goals and objectives?
<--- Score

5. Is there any additional endpoint protection solutions definition of success?
<--- Score

6. The political context: who holds power?
<--- Score

7. How do you gather the stories?
<--- Score

8. Has the improvement team collected the 'voice of the customer' (obtained feedback – qualitative and quantitative)?
<--- Score

9. What intelligence can you gather?
<--- Score

10. How do you keep key subject matter experts in the loop?
<--- Score

11. How will the endpoint protection solutions team and the group measure complete success of endpoint protection solutions?
<--- Score

12. Are the endpoint protection solutions requirements complete?
<--- Score

13. When are meeting minutes sent out? Who is on the distribution list?

<--- Score

14. Is there a clear endpoint protection solutions case definition?

<--- Score

15. Are resources adequate for the scope?

<--- Score

16. What is the scope of the endpoint protection solutions effort?

<--- Score

17. What was the context?

<--- Score

18. How was the 'as is' process map developed, reviewed, verified and validated?

<--- Score

19. How are consistent endpoint protection solutions definitions important?

<--- Score

20. What are the record-keeping requirements of endpoint protection solutions activities?

<--- Score

21. Is there regularly 100% attendance at the team meetings? If not, have appointed substitutes attended to preserve cross-functionality and full representation?

<--- Score

22. What are the Roles and Responsibilities for each team member and its leadership? Where is this documented?
<--- Score

23. Are there different segments of customers?
<--- Score

24. When is/was the endpoint protection solutions start date?
<--- Score

25. How is the team tracking and documenting its work?
<--- Score

26. What gets examined?
<--- Score

27. What customer feedback methods were used to solicit their input?
<--- Score

28. Is it clearly defined in and to your organization what you do?
<--- Score

29. Has the endpoint protection solutions work been fairly and/or equitably divided and delegated among team members who are qualified and capable to perform the work? Has everyone contributed?
<--- Score

30. Is the current 'as is' process being followed? If not, what are the discrepancies?

<--- Score

31. How do you hand over endpoint protection solutions context?
<--- Score

32. How did the endpoint protection solutions manager receive input to the development of a endpoint protection solutions improvement plan and the estimated completion dates/times of each activity?
<--- Score

33. How do you gather requirements?
<--- Score

34. What would be the goal or target for a endpoint protection solutions's improvement team?
<--- Score

35. Who is gathering information?
<--- Score

36. What is the definition of endpoint protection solutions excellence?
<--- Score

37. Is the scope of endpoint protection solutions defined?
<--- Score

38. Has the direction changed at all during the course of endpoint protection solutions? If so, when did it change and why?
<--- Score

39. Are there any constraints known that bear on the ability to perform endpoint protection solutions work? How is the team addressing them?
<--- Score

40. Is special endpoint protection solutions user knowledge required?
<--- Score

41. Is scope creep really all bad news?
<--- Score

42. What are the rough order estimates on cost savings/opportunities that endpoint protection solutions brings?
<--- Score

43. What baselines are required to be defined and managed?
<--- Score

44. Are task requirements clearly defined?
<--- Score

45. Who approved the endpoint protection solutions scope?
<--- Score

46. Why are you doing endpoint protection solutions and what is the scope?
<--- Score

47. Are audit criteria, scope, frequency and methods defined?
<--- Score

48. Is the improvement team aware of the different versions of a process: what they think it is vs. what it actually is vs. what it should be vs. what it could be?
<--- Score

49. Do you have a endpoint protection solutions success story or case study ready to tell and share?
<--- Score

50. Is the team adequately staffed with the desired cross-functionality? If not, what additional resources are available to the team?
<--- Score

51. What is the definition of success?
<--- Score

52. Do the problem and goal statements meet the SMART criteria (specific, measurable, attainable, relevant, and time-bound)?
<--- Score

53. Will a endpoint protection solutions production readiness review be required?
<--- Score

54. What are the requirements for audit information?
<--- Score

55. Have all basic functions of endpoint protection solutions been defined?
<--- Score

56. Has a team charter been developed and communicated?

<--- Score

57. What are (control) requirements for endpoint protection solutions Information?
<--- Score

58. Are different versions of process maps needed to account for the different types of inputs?
<--- Score

59. What are the compelling stakeholder reasons for embarking on endpoint protection solutions?
<--- Score

60. What is the context?
<--- Score

61. How do you manage changes in endpoint protection solutions requirements?
<--- Score

62. Has anyone else (internal or external to the group) attempted to solve this problem or a similar one before? If so, what knowledge can be leveraged from these previous efforts?
<--- Score

63. Has a project plan, Gantt chart, or similar been developed/completed?
<--- Score

64. How often are the team meetings?
<--- Score

65. How would you define the culture at your organization, how susceptible is it to endpoint

protection solutions changes?

<--- Score

66. How and when will the baselines be defined?

<--- Score

67. What is out of scope?

<--- Score

68. Who is gathering endpoint protection solutions information?

<--- Score

69. When is the estimated completion date?

<--- Score

70. Are approval levels defined for contracts and supplements to contracts?

<--- Score

71. How do you build the right business case?

<--- Score

72. Does the scope remain the same?

<--- Score

73. What scope do you want your strategy to cover?

<--- Score

74. Are the endpoint protection solutions requirements testable?

<--- Score

75. How do you manage unclear endpoint protection solutions requirements?

<--- Score

76. Has a high-level 'as is' process map been completed, verified and validated?
<--- Score

77. What defines best in class?
<--- Score

78. Does the team have regular meetings?
<--- Score

79. What is the worst case scenario?
<--- Score

80. In what way can you redefine the criteria of choice clients have in your category in your favor?
<--- Score

81. How do you manage scope?
<--- Score

82. What information should you gather?
<--- Score

83. What key stakeholder process output measure(s) does endpoint protection solutions leverage and how?
<--- Score

84. What information do you gather?
<--- Score

85. Who defines (or who defined) the rules and roles?
<--- Score

86. Has/have the customer(s) been identified?

<--- Score

87. How do you gather endpoint protection solutions requirements?
<--- Score

88. How do you catch endpoint protection solutions definition inconsistencies?
<--- Score

89. What endpoint protection solutions services do you require?
<--- Score

90. How can the value of endpoint protection solutions be defined?
<--- Score

91. Scope of sensitive information?
<--- Score

92. Is endpoint protection solutions required?
<--- Score

93. What critical content must be communicated – who, what, when, where, and how?
<--- Score

94. Have the customer needs been translated into specific, measurable requirements? How?
<--- Score

95. Are all requirements met?
<--- Score

96. What system do you use for gathering endpoint

protection solutions information?

<--- Score

97. What sources do you use to gather information for a endpoint protection solutions study?

<--- Score

98. How will variation in the actual durations of each activity be dealt with to ensure that the expected endpoint protection solutions results are met?

<--- Score

99. How would you define endpoint protection solutions leadership?

<--- Score

100. Is endpoint protection solutions currently on schedule according to the plan?

<--- Score

101. What is in scope?

<--- Score

102. What are the endpoint protection solutions use cases?

<--- Score

103. What are the boundaries of the scope? What is in bounds and what is not? What is the start point? What is the stop point?

<--- Score

104. Are required metrics defined, what are they?

<--- Score

105. What constraints exist that might impact the

team?
<--- Score

106. Is the work to date meeting requirements?
<--- Score

**107. Has a endpoint protection solutions
requirement not been met?**
<--- Score

108. Has your scope been defined?
<--- Score

109. How do you think the partners involved in
endpoint protection solutions would have defined
success?
<--- Score

110. Are accountability and ownership for endpoint
protection solutions clearly defined?
<--- Score

111. Are roles and responsibilities formally defined?
<--- Score

112. Is there a critical path to deliver endpoint
protection solutions results?
<--- Score

113. What are the tasks and definitions?
<--- Score

114. What endpoint protection solutions
requirements should be gathered?
<--- Score

115. What specifically is the problem? Where does it occur? When does it occur? What is its extent?
<--- Score

116. What happens if endpoint protection solutions's scope changes?
<--- Score

117. Do you all define endpoint protection solutions in the same way?
<--- Score

118. If substitutes have been appointed, have they been briefed on the endpoint protection solutions goals and received regular communications as to the progress to date?
<--- Score

119. What are the core elements of the endpoint protection solutions business case?
<--- Score

120. What is the scope of the endpoint protection solutions work?
<--- Score

121. Has everyone on the team, including the team leaders, been properly trained?
<--- Score

122. Who are the endpoint protection solutions improvement team members, including Management Leads and Coaches?
<--- Score

123. Have all of the relationships been defined

properly?
<--- Score

124. What scope to assess?
<--- Score

125. Is the endpoint protection solutions scope manageable?
<--- Score

126. How does the endpoint protection solutions manager ensure against scope creep?
<--- Score

127. What is the scope of endpoint protection solutions?
<--- Score

128. Have specific policy objectives been defined?
<--- Score

129. Is the endpoint protection solutions scope complete and appropriately sized?
<--- Score

130. What is in the scope and what is not in scope?
<--- Score

Add up total points for this section:
_ _ _ _ _ = Total points for this section

Divided by: _ _ _ _ _ _ (number of statements answered) = _ _ _ _ _ _
Average score for this section

Transfer your score to the endpoint

protection solutions Index at the beginning of the Self-Assessment.

CRITERION #3: MEASURE:

INTENT: Gather the correct data.
Measure the current performance and
evolution of the situation.

In my belief, the answer to this
question is clearly defined:

5 Strongly Agree

4 Agree

3 Neutral

2 Disagree

1 Strongly Disagree

1. How is progress measured?
<--- Score

2. What are the costs of reform?
<--- Score

3. At what cost?
<--- Score

4. Have you included everything in your endpoint protection solutions cost models?
<--- Score

5. How is the value delivered by endpoint protection solutions being measured?
<--- Score

6. What are the types and number of measures to use?
<--- Score

7. What causes extra work or rework?
<--- Score

8. How are costs allocated?
<--- Score

9. What causes innovation to fail or succeed in your organization?
<--- Score

10. What are allowable costs?
<--- Score

11. What is the cause of any endpoint protection solutions gaps?
<--- Score

12. Has a cost center been established?
<--- Score

13. What are the costs and benefits?
<--- Score

14. Are there any easy-to-implement alternatives to endpoint protection solutions? Sometimes other

solutions are available that do not require the cost implications of a full-blown project?
<--- Score

15. How can you manage cost down?
<--- Score

16. What would be a real cause for concern?
<--- Score

17. What causes mismanagement?
<--- Score

18. How do you verify if endpoint protection solutions is built right?
<--- Score

19. What are you verifying?
<--- Score

20. What is the endpoint protection solutions business impact?
<--- Score

21. How to cause the change?
<--- Score

22. What does your operating model cost?
<--- Score

23. Do you have an issue in getting priority?
<--- Score

24. Did you tackle the cause or the symptom?
<--- Score

25. What are the endpoint protection solutions key cost drivers?

<--- Score

26. How will effects be measured?

<--- Score

27. Are you able to realize any cost savings?

<--- Score

28. What would it cost to replace your technology?

<--- Score

29. Does the endpoint protection solutions task fit the client's priorities?

<--- Score

30. How can you measure endpoint protection solutions in a systematic way?

<--- Score

31. Where is the cost?

<--- Score

32. How do you verify the endpoint protection solutions requirements quality?

<--- Score

33. How frequently do you track endpoint protection solutions measures?

<--- Score

34. Is it possible to estimate the impact of unanticipated complexity such as wrong or failed assumptions, feedback, etcetera on proposed reforms?

<--- Score

35. How do you measure success?
<--- Score

36. How do you measure efficient delivery of endpoint protection solutions services?
<--- Score

37. What is the total cost related to deploying endpoint protection solutions, including any consulting or professional services?
<--- Score

38. Is the cost worth the endpoint protection solutions effort ?
<--- Score

39. Does management have the right priorities among projects?
<--- Score

40. What happens if cost savings do not materialize?
<--- Score

41. What are the costs?
<--- Score

42. What are your operating costs?
<--- Score

43. Are there competing endpoint protection solutions priorities?
<--- Score

44. Among the endpoint protection solutions

product and service cost to be estimated, which is considered hardest to estimate?

<--- Score

45. What are the strategic priorities for this year?

<--- Score

46. What is the root cause(s) of the problem?

<--- Score

47. Are actual costs in line with budgeted costs?

<--- Score

48. Who is involved in verifying compliance?

<--- Score

49. Are the measurements objective?

<--- Score

50. What are your primary costs, revenues, assets?

<--- Score

51. Who should receive measurement reports?

<--- Score

52. What are hidden endpoint protection solutions quality costs?

<--- Score

53. What disadvantage does this cause for the user?

<--- Score

54. What causes investor action?

<--- Score

55. What is your endpoint protection solutions quality

cost segregation study?
<--- Score

56. How will measures be used to manage and adapt?
<--- Score

57. How do you prevent mis-estimating cost?
<--- Score

58. Is there an opportunity to verify requirements?
<--- Score

59. What is the total fixed cost?
<--- Score

60. When a disaster occurs, who gets priority?
<--- Score

61. Why do the measurements/indicators matter?
<--- Score

62. Are indirect costs charged to the endpoint
protection solutions program?
<--- Score

63. How do you verify your resources?
<--- Score

64. Have you made assumptions about the shape of
the future, particularly its impact on your customers
and competitors?
<--- Score

65. Do you verify that corrective actions were taken?
<--- Score

66. How will your organization measure success?
<--- Score

67. What are the estimated costs of proposed changes?
<--- Score

68. Does a endpoint protection solutions quantification method exist?
<--- Score

69. What details are required of the endpoint protection solutions cost structure?
<--- Score

70. What tests verify requirements?
<--- Score

71. What do people want to verify?
<--- Score

72. What methods are feasible and acceptable to estimate the impact of reforms?
<--- Score

73. What relevant entities could be measured?
<--- Score

74. How can you reduce the costs of obtaining inputs?
<--- Score

75. What are the costs of delaying endpoint protection solutions action?
<--- Score

76. Do you effectively measure and reward individual

and team performance?
<--- Score

77. Where is it measured?
<--- Score

78. What is the cost of rework?
<--- Score

79. What drives O&M cost?
<--- Score

80. What is an unallowable cost?
<--- Score

81. What evidence is there and what is measured?
<--- Score

82. Are the endpoint protection solutions benefits worth its costs?
<--- Score

83. How are measurements made?
<--- Score

84. Do the benefits outweigh the costs?
<--- Score

85. What are the current costs of the endpoint protection solutions process?
<--- Score

86. Where can you go to verify the info?
<--- Score

87. How do your measurements capture actionable

endpoint protection solutions information for use in exceeding your customers expectations and securing your customers engagement?
<--- Score

88. What is your decision requirements diagram?
<--- Score

89. What potential environmental factors impact the endpoint protection solutions effort?
<--- Score

90. What does a Test Case verify?
<--- Score

91. How do you measure variability?
<--- Score

92. Which measures and indicators matter?
<   Score

93. How will you measure your endpoint protection solutions effectiveness?
<--- Score

94. Are missed endpoint protection solutions opportunities costing your organization money?
<--- Score

95. How do you aggregate measures across priorities?
<--- Score

96. Do you have a flow diagram of what happens?
<--- Score

97. How do you control the overall costs of your

work processes?
<--- Score

98. What measurements are being captured?
<--- Score

99. Which costs should be taken into account?
<--- Score

100. What does verifying compliance entail?
<--- Score

101. Are there measurements based on task performance?
<--- Score

102. Are you aware of what could cause a problem?
<--- Score

103. What are the operational costs after endpoint protection solutions deployment?
<--- Score

104. Who pays the cost?
<--- Score

105. Do you aggressively reward and promote the people who have the biggest impact on creating excellent endpoint protection solutions services/ products?
<--- Score

106. Are endpoint protection solutions vulnerabilities categorized and prioritized?
<--- Score

107. Do you have any cost endpoint protection solutions limitation requirements?
<--- Score

108. Have design-to-cost goals been established?
<--- Score

109. Why do you expend time and effort to implement measurement, for whom?
<--- Score

110. What could cause you to change course?
<--- Score

111. Will endpoint protection solutions have an impact on current business continuity, disaster recovery processes and/or infrastructure?
<--- Score

112. How will success or failure be measured?
<--- Score

113. How do you verify the authenticity of the data and information used?
<--- Score

114. Are you taking your company in the direction of better and revenue or cheaper and cost?
<--- Score

115. Is the solution cost-effective?
<--- Score

116. How do you verify and validate the endpoint protection solutions data?

<--- Score

117. Are supply costs steady or fluctuating?
<--- Score

118. Was a business case (cost/benefit) developed?
<--- Score

119. What is measured? Why?
<--- Score

120. How do you quantify and qualify impacts?
<--- Score

121. When should you bother with diagrams?
<--- Score

122. Are the units of measure consistent?
<--- Score

123. How do you verify and develop ideas and innovations?
<--- Score

124. What could cause delays in the schedule?
<--- Score

125. What are the endpoint protection solutions investment costs?
<--- Score

126. What measurements are possible, practicable and meaningful?
<--- Score

127. How do you verify performance?

<--- Score

128. How can you reduce costs?
<--- Score

129. How will costs be allocated?
<--- Score

130. How is performance measured?
<--- Score

131. What does losing customers cost your organization?
<--- Score

132. What are the uncertainties surrounding estimates of impact?
<--- Score

133. When are costs are incurred?
<--- Score

134. What harm might be caused?
<--- Score

Add up total points for this section:
_ _ _ _ _ = Total points for this section

Divided by: _ _ _ _ _ _ (number of statements answered) = _ _ _ _ _ _ Average score for this section

Transfer your score to the endpoint protection solutions Index at the beginning of the Self-Assessment.

CRITERION #4: ANALYZE:

INTENT: Analyze causes, assumptions and hypotheses.

In my belief, the answer to this question is clearly defined:

5 Strongly Agree

4 Agree

3 Neutral

2 Disagree

1 Strongly Disagree

1. Do you, as a leader, bounce back quickly from setbacks?
<--- Score

2. What are the necessary qualifications?
<--- Score

3. How many input/output points does it require?
<--- Score

4. What internal processes need improvement?
<--- Score

5. What conclusions were drawn from the team's data collection and analysis? How did the team reach these conclusions?
<--- Score

6. How do you ensure that the endpoint protection solutions opportunity is realistic?
<--- Score

7. What qualifications do endpoint protection solutions leaders need?
<--- Score

8. What qualifications are needed?
<--- Score

9. Was a detailed process map created to amplify critical steps of the 'as is' stakeholder process?
<--- Score

10. Is there an established change management process?
<--- Score

11. Has data output been validated?
<--- Score

12. How is the endpoint protection solutions Value Stream Mapping managed?
<--- Score

13. What other organizational variables, such as reward systems or communication systems, affect the

performance of this endpoint protection solutions process?
<--- Score

14. Are gaps between current performance and the goal performance identified?
<--- Score

15. What process should you select for improvement?
<--- Score

16. Think about the functions involved in your endpoint protection solutions project, what processes flow from these functions?
<--- Score

17. Are you missing endpoint protection solutions opportunities?
<--- Score

18. How has the endpoint protection solutions data been gathered?
<--- Score

19. What are the revised rough estimates of the financial savings/opportunity for endpoint protection solutions improvements?
<--- Score

20. How much data can be collected in the given timeframe?
<--- Score

21. Do you have the authority to produce the output?
<--- Score

22. Is the suppliers process defined and controlled?
<--- Score

23. What are your key performance measures or indicators and in-process measures for the control and improvement of your endpoint protection solutions processes?
<--- Score

24. Which endpoint protection solutions data should be retained?
<--- Score

25. How will the data be checked for quality?
<--- Score

26. Who will gather what data?
<--- Score

27. Was a cause-and-effect diagram used to explore the different types of causes (or sources of variation)?
<--- Score

28. Is pre-qualification of suppliers carried out?
<--- Score

29. What were the financial benefits resulting from any 'ground fruit or low-hanging fruit' (quick fixes)?
<--- Score

30. How was the detailed process map generated, verified, and validated?
<--- Score

31. Do your employees have the opportunity to do

what they do best everyday?
<--- Score

32. Is the gap/opportunity displayed and communicated in financial terms?
<--- Score

33. How do mission and objectives affect the endpoint protection solutions processes of your organization?
<--- Score

34. Identify an operational issue in your organization, for example, could a particular task be done more quickly or more efficiently by endpoint protection solutions?
<--- Score

35. Is the required endpoint protection solutions data gathered?
<--- Score

36. Have the problem and goal statements been updated to reflect the additional knowledge gained from the analyze phase?
<--- Score

37. Are all team members qualified for all tasks?
<--- Score

38. What other jobs or tasks affect the performance of the steps in the endpoint protection solutions process?
<--- Score

39. What endpoint protection solutions data should

be managed?
<--- Score

40. Were there any improvement opportunities identified from the process analysis?
<--- Score

41. Think about some of the processes you undertake within your organization, which do you own?
<--- Score

42. Have any additional benefits been identified that will result from closing all or most of the gaps?
<--- Score

43. How is data used for program management and improvement?
<--- Score

44. Do you understand your management processes today?
<--- Score

45. What resources go in to get the desired output?
<--- Score

46. What are your outputs?
<--- Score

47. Do staff qualifications match your project?
<--- Score

48. What is the complexity of the output produced?
<--- Score

49. How can risk management be tied procedurally

to process elements?
<--- Score

50. Who will facilitate the team and process?
<--- Score

51. How do you identify specific endpoint protection solutions investment opportunities and emerging trends?
<--- Score

52. Were any designed experiments used to generate additional insight into the data analysis?
<--- Score

53. How do you measure the operational performance of your key work systems and processes, including productivity, cycle time, and other appropriate measures of process effectiveness, efficiency, and innovation?
<--- Score

54. What are your endpoint protection solutions processes?
<--- Score

55. How will the change process be managed?
<--- Score

56. What controls do you have in place to protect data?
<--- Score

57. How do your work systems and key work processes relate to and capitalize on your core competencies?

<--- Score

58. How do you promote understanding that opportunity for improvement is not criticism of the status quo, or the people who created the status quo?
<--- Score

59. Should you invest in industry-recognized qualifications?
<--- Score

60. What qualifications and skills do you need?
<--- Score

61. Do several people in different organizational units assist with the endpoint protection solutions process?
<--- Score

62. How are outputs preserved and protected?
<--- Score

63. What do you need to qualify?
<--- Score

64. Are all staff in core endpoint protection solutions subjects Highly Qualified?
<--- Score

65. When should a process be art not science?
<--- Score

66. What quality tools were used to get through the analyze phase?
<--- Score

67. How do you use endpoint protection solutions

data and information to support organizational decision making and innovation?
<--- Score

68. How is endpoint protection solutions data gathered?
<--- Score

69. What tools were used to narrow the list of possible causes?
<--- Score

70. Is there a strict change management process?
<--- Score

71. How difficult is it to qualify what endpoint protection solutions ROI is?
<--- Score

72. Do your contracts/agreements contain data security obligations?
<--- Score

73. What output to create?
<--- Score

74. What types of data do your endpoint protection solutions indicators require?
<--- Score

75. What endpoint protection solutions metrics are outputs of the process?
<--- Score

76. Are your outputs consistent?
<--- Score

77. What is the cost of poor quality as supported by the team's analysis?
<--- Score

78. What are the best opportunities for value improvement?
<--- Score

79. Do your leaders quickly bounce back from setbacks?
<--- Score

80. Can you add value to the current endpoint protection solutions decision-making process (largely qualitative) by incorporating uncertainty modeling (more quantitative)?
<--- Score

81. What Is the Value Stream Mapping?
<--- Score

82. What are the disruptive endpoint protection solutions technologies that enable your organization to radically change your business processes?
<--- Score

83. Where is the data coming from to measure compliance?
<--- Score

84. How is the way you as the leader think and process information affecting your organizational culture?
<--- Score

85. What are your best practices for minimizing endpoint protection solutions project risk, while demonstrating incremental value and quick wins throughout the endpoint protection solutions project lifecycle?
<--- Score

86. Were Pareto charts (or similar) used to portray the 'heavy hitters' (or key sources of variation)?
<--- Score

87. What are your current levels and trends in key measures or indicators of endpoint protection solutions product and process performance that are important to and directly serve your customers? How do these results compare with the performance of your competitors and other organizations with similar offerings?
<--- Score

88. Record-keeping requirements flow from the records needed as inputs, outputs, controls and for transformation of a endpoint protection solutions process, are the records needed as inputs to the endpoint protection solutions process available?
<--- Score

89. What did the team gain from developing a sub-process map?
<--- Score

90. How do you implement and manage your work processes to ensure that they meet design requirements?
<--- Score

91. What are the endpoint protection solutions business drivers?

<--- Score

92. A compounding model resolution with available relevant data can often provide insight towards a solution methodology; which endpoint protection solutions models, tools and techniques are necessary?

<--- Score

93. What qualifications are necessary?

<--- Score

94. Who owns what data?

<--- Score

95. Is the performance gap determined?

<--- Score

96. What is the oversight process?

<--- Score

97. Where is endpoint protection solutions data gathered?

<--- Score

98. Are endpoint protection solutions changes recognized early enough to be approved through the regular process?

<--- Score

99. What is your organizations system for selecting qualified vendors?

<--- Score

100. Is the final output clearly identified?
<--- Score

101. What is the output?
<--- Score

102. What does the data say about the performance of the stakeholder process?
<--- Score

103. What were the crucial 'moments of truth' on the process map?
<--- Score

104. What kind of crime could a potential new hire have committed that would not only not disqualify him/her from being hired by your organization, but would actually indicate that he/she might be a particularly good fit?
<--- Score

105. What training and qualifications will you need?
<--- Score

106. Is data and process analysis, root cause analysis and quantifying the gap/opportunity in place?
<--- Score

107. Where can you get qualified talent today?
<--- Score

108. Did any value-added analysis or 'lean thinking' take place to identify some of the gaps shown on the 'as is' process map?
<--- Score

109. What process improvements will be needed?
<--- Score

110. Has an output goal been set?
<--- Score

111. Who gets your output?
<--- Score

112. What data do you need to collect?
<--- Score

113. How do you define collaboration and team output?
<--- Score

114. Do quality systems drive continuous improvement?
<--- Score

115. What information qualified as important?
<--- Score

116. What tools were used to generate the list of possible causes?
<--- Score

117. What endpoint protection solutions data should be collected?
<--- Score

118. Who qualifies to gain access to data?
<--- Score

119. What successful thing are you doing today that

may be blinding you to new growth opportunities?
<--- Score

120. What qualifies as competition?
<--- Score

121. Is the endpoint protection solutions process severely broken such that a re-design is necessary?
<--- Score

122. What are the processes for audit reporting and management?
<--- Score

123. How does the organization define, manage, and improve its endpoint protection solutions processes?
<--- Score

124. Did any additional data need to be collected?
<--- Score

125. What are your current levels and trends in key endpoint protection solutions measures or indicators of product and process performance that are important to and directly serve your customers?
<--- Score

126. What data is gathered?
<--- Score

127. An organizationally feasible system request is one that considers the mission, goals and objectives of the organization, key questions are: is the endpoint protection solutions solution request practical and will it solve a problem or take advantage of an opportunity to achieve company goals?

<--- Score

128. Have you defined which data is gathered how?

<--- Score

129. What, related to, endpoint protection solutions processes does your organization outsource?

<--- Score

130. Who is involved in the management review process?

<--- Score

Add up total points for this section:
_ _ _ _ _ = Total points for this section

Divided by: _ _ _ _ _ _ (number of statements answered) = _ _ _ _ _ _
Average score for this section

Transfer your score to the endpoint protection solutions Index at the beginning of the Self-Assessment.

CRITERION #5: IMPROVE:

INTENT: Develop a practical solution. Innovate, establish and test the solution and to measure the results.

In my belief, the answer to this question is clearly defined:

5 Strongly Agree

4 Agree

3 Neutral

2 Disagree

1 Strongly Disagree

1. Who are the endpoint protection solutions decision-makers?
<--- Score

2. What went well, what should change, what can improve?
<--- Score

3. What to do with the results or outcomes of

measurements?
<--- Score

4. Where do you need endpoint protection solutions improvement?
<--- Score

5. How will you know that a change is an improvement?
<--- Score

6. What endpoint protection solutions improvements can be made?
<--- Score

7. What tools were used to evaluate the potential solutions?
<--- Score

8. Is the solution technically practical?
<--- Score

9. If you could go back in time five years, what decision would you make differently? What is your best guess as to what decision you're making today you might regret five years from now?
<--- Score

10. Where do the endpoint protection solutions decisions reside?
<--- Score

11. Does a good decision guarantee a good outcome?
<--- Score

12. For estimation problems, how do you develop an

estimation statement?

<--- Score

13. endpoint protection solutions risk decisions: whose call Is It?

<--- Score

14. Who controls the risk?

<--- Score

15. How can you better manage risk?

<--- Score

16. How do the endpoint protection solutions results compare with the performance of your competitors and other organizations with similar offerings?

<--- Score

17. How do you improve endpoint protection solutions service perception, and satisfaction?

<--- Score

18. Are events managed to resolution?

<--- Score

19. What lessons, if any, from a pilot were incorporated into the design of the full-scale solution?

<--- Score

20. Do you cover the five essential competencies: Communication, Collaboration,Innovation, Adaptability, and Leadership that improve an organizations ability to leverage the new endpoint protection solutions in a volatile global economy?

<--- Score

21. Do vendor agreements bring new compliance risk ?

<--- Score

22. Who will be responsible for making the decisions to include or exclude requested changes once endpoint protection solutions is underway?

<--- Score

23. What should a proof of concept or pilot accomplish?

<--- Score

24. What are the concrete endpoint protection solutions results?

<--- Score

25. Have you achieved endpoint protection solutions improvements?

<--- Score

26. Are the most efficient solutions problem-specific?

<--- Score

27. Who controls key decisions that will be made?

<--- Score

28. How are policy decisions made and where?

<--- Score

29. How does the team improve its work?

<--- Score

30. What are your current levels and trends in key measures or indicators of workforce and leader development?

<--- Score

31. How will you know when its improved?
<--- Score

32. How do you measure risk?
<--- Score

33. What do you want to improve?
<--- Score

34. Is there any other endpoint protection solutions solution?
<--- Score

35. How is knowledge sharing about risk management improved?
<--- Score

36. Who will be using the results of the measurement activities?
<--- Score

37. Does the goal represent a desired result that can be measured?
<--- Score

38. What actually has to improve and by how much?
<--- Score

39. Are decisions made in a timely manner?
<--- Score

40. Are risk management tasks balanced centrally and locally?
<--- Score

41. Is endpoint protection solutions documentation maintained?
<--- Score

42. How do you improve your likelihood of success ?
<--- Score

43. What does the 'should be' process map/design look like?
<--- Score

44. How will you recognize and celebrate results?
<--- Score

45. What is the magnitude of the improvements?
<--- Score

46. What tools do you use once you have decided on a endpoint protection solutions strategy and more importantly how do you choose?
<--- Score

47. Is the measure of success for endpoint protection solutions understandable to a variety of people?
<--- Score

48. What practices helps your organization to develop its capacity to recognize patterns?
<--- Score

49. How do you manage and improve your endpoint protection solutions work systems to deliver customer value and achieve organizational success and sustainability?
<--- Score

50. For decision problems, how do you develop a decision statement?
<--- Score

51. What risks do you need to manage?
<--- Score

52. What attendant changes will need to be made to ensure that the solution is successful?
<--- Score

53. Are risk triggers captured?
<--- Score

54. What were the underlying assumptions on the cost-benefit analysis?
<--- Score

55. To what extent does management recognize endpoint protection solutions as a tool to increase the results?
<--- Score

56. What is the endpoint protection solutions's sustainability risk?
<--- Score

57. How can the phases of endpoint protection solutions development be identified?
<--- Score

58. Is any endpoint protection solutions documentation required?
<--- Score

59. How do you measure progress and evaluate training effectiveness?

<--- Score

60. Who should make the endpoint protection solutions decisions?

<--- Score

61. How does your organization evaluate strategic endpoint protection solutions success?

<--- Score

62. What communications are necessary to support the implementation of the solution?

<--- Score

63. Is there a high likelihood that any recommendations will achieve their intended results?

<--- Score

64. What is endpoint protection solutions's impact on utilizing the best solution(s)?

<--- Score

65. How scalable is your endpoint protection solutions solution?

<--- Score

66. What needs improvement? Why?

<--- Score

67. What is the implementation plan?

<--- Score

68. How risky is your organization?

<--- Score

69. How do you deal with endpoint protection
solutions risk?
<--- Score

**70. When you map the key players in your own
work and the types/domains of relationships with
them, which relationships do you find easy and
which challenging, and why?**
<--- Score

71. In the past few months, what is the smallest
change you have made that has had the biggest
positive result? What was it about that small change
that produced the large return?
<--- Score

**72. How do you manage endpoint protection
solutions risk?**
<--- Score

73. Can you integrate quality management and risk
management?
<--- Score

74. Are the key business and technology risks being
managed?
<--- Score

**75. Can you identify any significant risks or
exposures to endpoint protection solutions
third- parties (vendors, service providers, alliance
partners etc) that concern you?**
<--- Score

76. Do you have the optimal project management

team structure?
<--- Score

77. Who manages supplier risk management in your organization?
<--- Score

78. How can skill-level changes improve endpoint protection solutions?
<--- Score

79. Who are the key stakeholders for the endpoint protection solutions evaluation?
<--- Score

80. How do you define the solutions' scope?
<--- Score

81. What criteria will you use to assess your endpoint protection solutions risks?
<--- Score

82. How will you know that you have improved?
<--- Score

83. How do you go about comparing endpoint protection solutions approaches/solutions?
<--- Score

84. What are the affordable endpoint protection solutions risks?
<--- Score

85. Risk Identification: What are the possible risk events your organization faces in relation to endpoint protection solutions?

<--- Score

86. Can the solution be designed and implemented within an acceptable time period?
<--- Score

87. Is the scope clearly documented?
<--- Score

88. Are procedures documented for managing endpoint protection solutions risks?
<--- Score

89. Are the risks fully understood, reasonable and manageable?
<--- Score

90. What assumptions are made about the solution and approach?
<--- Score

91. How is continuous improvement applied to risk management?
<--- Score

92. Do those selected for the endpoint protection solutions team have a good general understanding of what endpoint protection solutions is all about?
<--- Score

93. What improvements have been achieved?
<--- Score

94. Why improve in the first place?
<--- Score

95. How are endpoint protection solutions risks managed?

<--- Score

96. Is the endpoint protection solutions documentation thorough?

<--- Score

97. Who are the endpoint protection solutions decision makers?

<--- Score

98. How do you link measurement and risk?

<--- Score

99. Is the endpoint protection solutions risk managed?

<--- Score

100. Who are the people involved in developing and implementing endpoint protection solutions?

<--- Score

101. Which of the recognised risks out of all risks can be most likely transferred?

<--- Score

102. How significant is the improvement in the eyes of the end user?

<--- Score

103. Who will be responsible for documenting the endpoint protection solutions requirements in detail?

<--- Score

104. Explorations of the frontiers of endpoint protection solutions will help you build influence, improve endpoint protection solutions, optimize decision making, and sustain change, what is your approach?

<--- Score

105. What tools were most useful during the improve phase?

<--- Score

106. What is the risk?

<--- Score

107. What resources are required for the improvement efforts?

<--- Score

108. Is the implementation plan designed?

<--- Score

109. Risk factors: what are the characteristics of endpoint protection solutions that make it risky?

<--- Score

110. How do you decide how much to remunerate an employee?

<--- Score

111. Have you identified breakpoints and/or risk tolerances that will trigger broad consideration of a potential need for intervention or modification of strategy?

<--- Score

112. Is the optimal solution selected based on testing

and analysis?
<--- Score

113. Was a pilot designed for the proposed solution(s)?
<--- Score

114. Is there a cost/benefit analysis of optimal solution(s)?
<--- Score

115. How do you mitigate endpoint protection solutions risk?
<--- Score

116. How will you measure the results?
<--- Score

117. Is risk periodically assessed?
<--- Score

118. Risk events: what are the things that could go wrong?
<--- Score

119. Who makes the endpoint protection solutions decisions in your organization?
<--- Score

120. Who manages endpoint protection solutions risk?
<--- Score

121. What is the team's contingency plan for potential problems occurring in implementation?
<--- Score

122. Were any criteria developed to assist the team in testing and evaluating potential solutions?
<--- Score

123. What can you do to improve?
<--- Score

124. Who do you report endpoint protection solutions results to?
<--- Score

125. What tools were used to tap into the creativity and encourage 'outside the box' thinking?
<--- Score

126. Is there a small-scale pilot for proposed improvement(s)? What conclusions were drawn from the outcomes of a pilot?
<--- Score

127. What strategies for endpoint protection solutions improvement are successful?
<--- Score

128. Are you assessing endpoint protection solutions and risk?
<--- Score

129. What are the expected endpoint protection solutions results?
<--- Score

130. How do you improve productivity?
<--- Score

131. What error proofing will be done to address some of the discrepancies observed in the 'as is' process?
<--- Score

132. How do you measure improved endpoint protection solutions service perception, and satisfaction?
<--- Score

133. What are the endpoint protection solutions security risks?
<--- Score

134. Was a endpoint protection solutions charter developed?
<--- Score

135. How can you improve endpoint protection solutions?
<--- Score

136. What were the criteria for evaluating a endpoint protection solutions pilot?
<--- Score

137. Do you need to do a usability evaluation?
<--- Score

138. What current systems have to be understood and/or changed?
<--- Score

139. Is supporting endpoint protection solutions documentation required?
<--- Score

140. At what point will vulnerability assessments be performed once endpoint protection solutions is put into production (e.g., ongoing Risk Management after implementation)?
<--- Score

Add up total points for this section:
_ _ _ _ _ = Total points for this section

Divided by: _ _ _ _ _ _ (number of statements answered) = _ _ _ _ _ _
Average score for this section

Transfer your score to the endpoint protection solutions Index at the beginning of the Self-Assessment.

CRITERION #6: CONTROL:

INTENT: Implement the practical solution. Maintain the performance and correct possible complications.

In my belief, the answer to this question is clearly defined:

5 Strongly Agree

4 Agree

3 Neutral

2 Disagree

1 Strongly Disagree

1. Are suggested corrective/restorative actions indicated on the response plan for known causes to problems that might surface?
<--- Score

2. Are the endpoint protection solutions standards challenging?
<--- Score

3. What should the next improvement project be that is related to endpoint protection solutions?
<--- Score

4. Are controls in place and consistently applied?
<--- Score

5. What are you attempting to measure/monitor?
<--- Score

6. How will the process owner and team be able to hold the gains?
<--- Score

7. What is the standard for acceptable endpoint protection solutions performance?
<--- Score

8. Is a response plan in place for when the input, process, or output measures indicate an 'out-of-control' condition?
<--- Score

9. Are operating procedures consistent?
<--- Score

10. Is a response plan established and deployed?
<--- Score

11. How will you measure your QA plan's effectiveness?
<--- Score

12. How will endpoint protection solutions decisions be made and monitored?
<--- Score

13. What is the control/monitoring plan?
<--- Score

14. Are you measuring, monitoring and predicting endpoint protection solutions activities to optimize operations and profitability, and enhancing outcomes?
<--- Score

15. Do you monitor the effectiveness of your endpoint protection solutions activities?
<--- Score

16. How will the day-to-day responsibilities for monitoring and continual improvement be transferred from the improvement team to the process owner?
<--- Score

17. Are new process steps, standards, and documentation ingrained into normal operations?
<--- Score

18. How is endpoint protection solutions project cost planned, managed, monitored?
<--- Score

19. Has the improved process and its steps been standardized?
<--- Score

20. What quality tools were useful in the control phase?
<--- Score

21. Is reporting being used or needed?
<--- Score

22. You may have created your quality measures at a time when you lacked resources, technology wasn't up to the required standard, or low service levels were the industry norm. Have those circumstances changed?
<--- Score

23. How will input, process, and output variables be checked to detect for sub-optimal conditions?
<--- Score

24. Is there a transfer of ownership and knowledge to process owner and process team tasked with the responsibilities.
<--- Score

25. How do you spread information?
<--- Score

26. Is knowledge gained on process shared and institutionalized?
<--- Score

27. Is there a endpoint protection solutions Communication plan covering who needs to get what information when?
<--- Score

28. Act/Adjust: What Do you Need to Do Differently?
<--- Score

29. Does job training on the documented procedures need to be part of the process team's education and

training?
<--- Score

30. What do you measure to verify effectiveness gains?
<--- Score

31. What do you stand for--and what are you against?
<--- Score

32. Are the planned controls working?
<--- Score

33. In the case of a endpoint protection solutions project, the criteria for the audit derive from implementation objectives, an audit of a endpoint protection solutions project involves assessing whether the recommendations outlined for implementation have been met, can you track that any endpoint protection solutions project is implemented as planned, and is it working?
<--- Score

34. Will your goals reflect your program budget?
<--- Score

35. Will any special training be provided for results interpretation?
<--- Score

36. Do you monitor the endpoint protection solutions decisions made and fine tune them as they evolve?
<--- Score

37. What adjustments to the strategies are needed?
<--- Score

38. How likely is the current endpoint protection solutions plan to come in on schedule or on budget?
<--- Score

39. How will new or emerging customer needs/ requirements be checked/communicated to orient the process toward meeting the new specifications and continually reducing variation?
<--- Score

40. Who controls critical resources?
<--- Score

41. How widespread is its use?
<--- Score

42. Who will be in control?
<--- Score

43. What are the key elements of your endpoint protection solutions performance improvement system, including your evaluation, organizational learning, and innovation processes?
<--- Score

44. What is your theory of human motivation, and how does your compensation plan fit with that view?
<--- Score

45. Is there a standardized process?
<--- Score

46. Is there documentation that will support the successful operation of the improvement?

<--- Score

47. Is there an action plan in case of emergencies?
<--- Score

48. Does a troubleshooting guide exist or is it needed?
<--- Score

49. How do you select, collect, align, and integrate endpoint protection solutions data and information for tracking daily operations and overall organizational performance, including progress relative to strategic objectives and action plans?
<--- Score

50. What are the critical parameters to watch?
<--- Score

51. Is there a recommended audit plan for routine surveillance inspections of endpoint protection solutions's gains?
<--- Score

52. Are the planned controls in place?
<--- Score

53. Is there a documented and implemented monitoring plan?
<--- Score

54. Is there a control plan in place for sustaining improvements (short and long-term)?
<--- Score

55. What can you control?
<--- Score

56. Has the endpoint protection solutions value of standards been quantified?
<--- Score

57. Are there documented procedures?
<--- Score

58. Who is the endpoint protection solutions process owner?
<--- Score

59. How can you best use all of your knowledge repositories to enhance learning and sharing?
<--- Score

60. What other areas of the group might benefit from the endpoint protection solutions team's improvements, knowledge, and learning?
<--- Score

61. Where do ideas that reach policy makers and planners as proposals for endpoint protection solutions strengthening and reform actually originate?
<--- Score

62. Who sets the endpoint protection solutions standards?
<--- Score

63. How do you encourage people to take control and responsibility?
<--- Score

64. How might the group capture best practices and

lessons learned so as to leverage improvements?
<--- Score

65. What is the recommended frequency of auditing?
<--- Score

66. What should you measure to verify efficiency gains?
<--- Score

67. Is new knowledge gained imbedded in the response plan?
<--- Score

68. What are the performance and scale of the endpoint protection solutions tools?
<--- Score

69. How do you plan for the cost of succession?
<--- Score

70. Have new or revised work instructions resulted?
<--- Score

71. Are documented procedures clear and easy to follow for the operators?
<--- Score

72. What key inputs and outputs are being measured on an ongoing basis?
<--- Score

73. Are pertinent alerts monitored, analyzed and distributed to appropriate personnel?
<--- Score

74. What do your reports reflect?

<--- Score

75. Who has control over resources?

<--- Score

76. Against what alternative is success being measured?

<--- Score

77. What are the known security controls?

<--- Score

78. Implementation Planning: is a pilot needed to test the changes before a full roll out occurs?

<--- Score

79. What are your results for key measures or indicators of the accomplishment of your endpoint protection solutions strategy and action plans, including building and strengthening core competencies?

<--- Score

80. Does the response plan contain a definite closed loop continual improvement scheme (e.g., plan-do-check-act)?

<--- Score

81. What endpoint protection solutions standards are applicable?

<--- Score

82. Does the endpoint protection solutions performance meet the customer's requirements?

<--- Score

83. How is change control managed?
<--- Score

84. How do senior leaders actions reflect a commitment to the organizations endpoint protection solutions values?
<--- Score

85. Does endpoint protection solutions appropriately measure and monitor risk?
<--- Score

86. Who is going to spread your message?
<--- Score

87. What is your plan to assess your security risks?
<--- Score

88. Do the endpoint protection solutions decisions you make today help people and the planet tomorrow?
<--- Score

89. How will report readings be checked to effectively monitor performance?
<--- Score

90. Do the viable solutions scale to future needs?
<--- Score

91. How do your controls stack up?
<--- Score

92. How do you establish and deploy modified action plans if circumstances require a shift in plans and

rapid execution of new plans?
<--- Score

93. What other systems, operations, processes, and infrastructures (hiring practices, staffing, training, incentives/rewards, metrics/dashboards/scorecards, etc.) need updates, additions, changes, or deletions in order to facilitate knowledge transfer and improvements?
<--- Score

94. How do controls support value?
<--- Score

95. What are customers monitoring?
<--- Score

96. How do you plan on providing proper recognition and disclosure of supporting companies?
<--- Score

97. Is the endpoint protection solutions test/ monitoring cost justified?
<--- Score

98. Can support from partners be adjusted?
<--- Score

99. How will the process owner verify improvement in present and future sigma levels, process capabilities?
<--- Score

Add up total points for this section:
_____ = Total points for this section

Divided by: _____ (number of

statements answered) = _____
Average score for this section

Transfer your score to the endpoint protection solutions Index at the beginning of the Self-Assessment.

CRITERION #7: SUSTAIN:

INTENT: Retain the benefits.

In my belief, the answer to this question is clearly defined:

5 Strongly Agree

4 Agree

3 Neutral

2 Disagree

1 Strongly Disagree

1. Who do you think the world wants your organization to be?
<--- Score

2. Operational - will it work?
<--- Score

3. What will be the consequences to the stakeholder (financial, reputation etc) if endpoint protection solutions does not go ahead or fails to deliver the objectives?

<--- Score

4. Who will provide the final approval of endpoint protection solutions deliverables?
<--- Score

5. Are there any activities that you can take off your to do list?
<--- Score

6. Were lessons learned captured and communicated?
<--- Score

7. What have been your experiences in defining long range endpoint protection solutions goals?
<--- Score

8. How do you listen to customers to obtain actionable information?
<--- Score

9. How can you negotiate endpoint protection solutions successfully with a stubborn boss, an irate client, or a deceitful coworker?
<--- Score

10. How will you know that the endpoint protection solutions project has been successful?
<--- Score

11. What is the overall business strategy?
<--- Score

12. Are your responses positive or negative?
<--- Score

13. What unique value proposition (UVP) do you offer?
<--- Score

14. Who will be responsible for deciding whether endpoint protection solutions goes ahead or not after the initial investigations?
<--- Score

15. To whom do you add value?
<--- Score

16. If you had to leave your organization for a year and the only communication you could have with employees/colleagues was a single paragraph, what would you write?
<--- Score

17. Think of your endpoint protection solutions project, what are the main functions?
<--- Score

18. How likely is it that a customer would recommend your company to a friend or colleague?
<--- Score

19. What is effective endpoint protection solutions?
<--- Score

20. Will it be accepted by users?
<--- Score

21. Can the schedule be done in the given time?
<--- Score

22. Are new benefits received and understood?

<--- Score

23. Who will manage the integration of tools?
<--- Score

24. How do you manage endpoint protection solutions Knowledge Management (KM)?
<--- Score

25. How do you transition from the baseline to the target?
<--- Score

26. Are all key stakeholders present at all Structured Walkthroughs?
<--- Score

27. Political -is anyone trying to undermine this project?
<--- Score

28. How do you govern and fulfill your societal responsibilities?
<--- Score

29. How is implementation research currently incorporated into each of your goals?
<--- Score

30. How do you assess the endpoint protection solutions pitfalls that are inherent in implementing it?
<--- Score

31. What are specific endpoint protection solutions rules to follow?
<--- Score

32. Which functions and people interact with the supplier and or customer?
<--- Score

33. Who is responsible for endpoint protection solutions?
<--- Score

34. What are your personal philosophies regarding endpoint protection solutions and how do they influence your work?
<--- Score

35. What is something you believe that nearly no one agrees with you on?
<--- Score

36. What happens when a new employee joins the organization?
<--- Score

37. Which endpoint protection solutions goals are the most important?
<--- Score

38. How important is endpoint protection solutions to the user organizations mission?
<--- Score

39. How do you keep records, of what?
<--- Score

40. Marketing budgets are tighter, consumers are more skeptical, and social media has changed forever the way we talk about endpoint protection solutions,

how do you gain traction?
<--- Score

41. Why should you adopt a endpoint protection solutions framework?
<--- Score

42. What stupid rule would you most like to kill?
<--- Score

43. How do you cross-sell and up-sell your endpoint protection solutions success?
<--- Score

44. How do customers see your organization?
<--- Score

45. Who is the main stakeholder, with ultimate responsibility for driving endpoint protection solutions forward?
<--- Score

46. How are you doing compared to your industry?
<--- Score

47. What is the big endpoint protection solutions idea?
<--- Score

48. What goals did you miss?
<--- Score

49. How much does endpoint protection solutions help?
<--- Score

50. What is a feasible sequencing of reform initiatives over time?
<--- Score

51. In retrospect, of the projects that you pulled the plug on, what percent do you wish had been allowed to keep going, and what percent do you wish had ended earlier?
<--- Score

52. What is the estimated value of the project?
<--- Score

53. How do you make it meaningful in connecting endpoint protection solutions with what users do day-to-day?
<--- Score

54. Do you feel that more should be done in the endpoint protection solutions area?
<--- Score

55. What are the usability implications of endpoint protection solutions actions?
<--- Score

56. Is endpoint protection solutions realistic, or are you setting yourself up for failure?
<--- Score

57. What could happen if you do not do it?
<--- Score

58. What is the craziest thing you can do?
<--- Score

59. Do you know who is a friend or a foe?
<--- Score

60. If your customer were your grandmother, would you tell her to buy what you're selling?
<--- Score

61. In a project to restructure endpoint protection solutions outcomes, which stakeholders would you involve?
<--- Score

62. Is it economical; do you have the time and money?
<--- Score

63. Who is responsible for ensuring appropriate resources (time, people and money) are allocated to endpoint protection solutions?
<--- Score

64. Is a endpoint protection solutions team work effort in place?
<--- Score

65. Which individuals, teams or departments will be involved in endpoint protection solutions?
<--- Score

66. How can you become more high-tech but still be high touch?
<--- Score

67. What projects are going on in the organization today, and what resources are those projects using from the resource pools?
<--- Score

68. What is your competitive advantage?
<--- Score

69. If you had to rebuild your organization without any traditional competitive advantages (i.e., no killer technology, promising research, innovative product/service delivery model, etcetera), how would your people have to approach their work and collaborate together in order to create the necessary conditions for success?
<--- Score

70. If your company went out of business tomorrow, would anyone who doesn't get a paycheck here care?
<--- Score

71. What are the essentials of internal endpoint protection solutions management?
<--- Score

72. What new services of functionality will be implemented next with endpoint protection solutions ?
<--- Score

73. Would you rather sell to knowledgeable and informed customers or to uninformed customers?
<--- Score

74. Do you have enough freaky customers in your portfolio pushing you to the limit day in and day out?
<--- Score

75. Who uses your product in ways you never expected?

<--- Score

76. How do you accomplish your long range endpoint protection solutions goals?
<--- Score

77. Who have you, as a company, historically been when you've been at your best?
<--- Score

78. What are the rules and assumptions your industry operates under? What if the opposite were true?
<--- Score

79. What is the kind of project structure that would be appropriate for your endpoint protection solutions project, should it be formal and complex, or can it be less formal and relatively simple?
<--- Score

80. How do you provide a safe environment -physically and emotionally?
<--- Score

81. What are the short and long-term endpoint protection solutions goals?
<--- Score

82. Whose voice (department, ethnic group, women, older workers, etc) might you have missed hearing from in your company, and how might you amplify this voice to create positive momentum for your business?
<--- Score

83. Are you making progress, and are you making

progress as endpoint protection solutions leaders?
<--- Score

84. What one word do you want to own in the minds of your customers, employees, and partners?
<--- Score

85. Do you have an implicit bias for capital investments over people investments?
<--- Score

86. How do you deal with endpoint protection solutions changes?
<--- Score

87. How do you foster innovation?
<--- Score

88. Are you changing as fast as the world around you?
<--- Score

89. What are the long-term endpoint protection solutions goals?
<--- Score

90. What would have to be true for the option on the table to be the best possible choice?
<--- Score

91. What you are going to do to affect the numbers?
<--- Score

92. How will you insure seamless interoperability of endpoint protection solutions moving forward?

<--- Score

93. What trouble can you get into?
<--- Score

94. What are your most important goals for the strategic endpoint protection solutions objectives?
<--- Score

95. What relationships among endpoint protection solutions trends do you perceive?
<--- Score

96. How much contingency will be available in the budget?
<--- Score

97. Who are your customers?
<--- Score

98. What are the top 3 things at the forefront of your endpoint protection solutions agendas for the next 3 years?
<--- Score

99. Are you using a design thinking approach and integrating Innovation, endpoint protection solutions Experience, and Brand Value?
<--- Score

100. Where can you break convention?
<--- Score

101. What is your formula for success in endpoint protection solutions ?
<--- Score

102. What threat is endpoint protection solutions addressing?
<--- Score

103. How do you lead with endpoint protection solutions in mind?
<--- Score

104. What do we do when new problems arise?
<--- Score

105. Is endpoint protection solutions dependent on the successful delivery of a current project?
<--- Score

106. Do you think endpoint protection solutions accomplishes the goals you expect it to accomplish?
<--- Score

107. How do you stay inspired?
<--- Score

108. What are current endpoint protection solutions paradigms?
<--- Score

109. Do you know what you are doing? And who do you call if you don't?
<--- Score

110. What counts that you are not counting?
<--- Score

111. How do you ensure that implementations of endpoint protection solutions products are done in a

way that ensures safety?
<--- Score

112. How do you engage the workforce, in addition to satisfying them?
<--- Score

113. What have you done to protect your business from competitive encroachment?
<--- Score

114. What was the last experiment you ran?
<--- Score

115. What is the funding source for this project?
<--- Score

116. Can you break it down?
<--- Score

117. If no one would ever find out about your accomplishments, how would you lead differently?
<--- Score

118. What is your endpoint protection solutions strategy?
<--- Score

119. How do you keep the momentum going?
<--- Score

120. Why do and why don't your customers like your organization?
<--- Score

121. What is the range of capabilities?

<--- Score

122. How do you determine the key elements that affect endpoint protection solutions workforce satisfaction, how are these elements determined for different workforce groups and segments?
<--- Score

123. What are you challenging?
<--- Score

124. Do you see more potential in people than they do in themselves?
<--- Score

125. What does your signature ensure?
<--- Score

126. What information is critical to your organization that your executives are ignoring?
<--- Score

127. Do you think you know, or do you know you know ?
<--- Score

128. What happens at your organization when people fail?
<--- Score

129. Do you have past endpoint protection solutions successes?
<--- Score

130. Are the criteria for selecting recommendations stated?

<--- Score

131. How do you create buy-in?
<--- Score

132. What is an unauthorized commitment?
<--- Score

133. Is the impact that endpoint protection solutions has shown?
<--- Score

134. Who else should you help?
<--- Score

135. How do senior leaders deploy your organizations vision and values through your leadership system, to the workforce, to key suppliers and partners, and to customers and other stakeholders, as appropriate?
<--- Score

136. Is there any existing endpoint protection solutions governance structure?
<--- Score

137. Do you have the right capabilities and capacities?
<--- Score

138. Can you do all this work?
<--- Score

139. Who are the key stakeholders?
<--- Score

140. What are the potential basics of endpoint protection solutions fraud?

<--- Score

141. Is your basic point _____ or _____?
<--- Score

142. Who, on the executive team or the board, has spoken to a customer recently?
<--- Score

143. If you find that you havent accomplished one of the goals for one of the steps of the endpoint protection solutions strategy, what will you do to fix it?
<--- Score

144. Why should people listen to you?
<--- Score

145. What must you excel at?
<--- Score

146. Instead of going to current contacts for new ideas, what if you reconnected with dormant contacts--the people you used to know? If you were going reactivate a dormant tie, who would it be?
<--- Score

147. If you do not follow, then how to lead?
<--- Score

148. What is your question? Why?
<--- Score

149. What are the gaps in your knowledge and experience?
<--- Score

150. Which models, tools and techniques are necessary?

<--- Score

151. Are you relevant? Will you be relevant five years from now? Ten?

<--- Score

152. Why will customers want to buy your organizations products/services?

<--- Score

153. Is a endpoint protection solutions breakthrough on the horizon?

<--- Score

154. Has implementation been effective in reaching specified objectives so far?

<--- Score

155. If you weren't already in this business, would you enter it today? And if not, what are you going to do about it?

<--- Score

156. What are strategies for increasing support and reducing opposition?

<--- Score

157. Do you have the right people on the bus?

<--- Score

158. What trophy do you want on your mantle?

<--- Score

159. How will you ensure you get what you expected?
<--- Score

160. What business benefits will endpoint protection solutions goals deliver if achieved?
<--- Score

161. What may be the consequences for the performance of an organization if all stakeholders are not consulted regarding endpoint protection solutions?
<--- Score

162. How do you set endpoint protection solutions stretch targets and how do you get people to not only participate in setting these stretch targets but also that they strive to achieve these?
<--- Score

163. What is the recommended frequency of auditing?
<--- Score

164. When information truly is ubiquitous, when reach and connectivity are completely global, when computing resources are infinite, and when a whole new set of impossibilities are not only possible, but happening, what will that do to your business?
<--- Score

165. How can you incorporate support to ensure safe and effective use of endpoint protection solutions into the services that you provide?
<--- Score

166. Have new benefits been realized?

<--- Score

167. Who is responsible for errors?
<--- Score

168. How does endpoint protection solutions integrate with other stakeholder initiatives?
<--- Score

169. What is it like to work for you?
<--- Score

170. Why not do endpoint protection solutions?
<--- Score

171. Are assumptions made in endpoint protection solutions stated explicitly?
<--- Score

172. What is the purpose of endpoint protection solutions in relation to the mission?
<--- Score

173. At what moment would you think; Will I get fired?
<--- Score

174. Do endpoint protection solutions rules make a reasonable demand on a users capabilities?
<--- Score

175. Do you say no to customers for no reason?
<--- Score

176. Did your employees make progress today?
<--- Score

177. What are the challenges?
<--- Score

178. What are you trying to prove to yourself, and how might it be hijacking your life and business success?
<--- Score

179. What potential megatrends could make your business model obsolete?
<--- Score

180. What are the business goals endpoint protection solutions is aiming to achieve?
<--- Score

181. What did you miss in the interview for the worst hire you ever made?
<--- Score

182. Are the assumptions believable and achievable?
<--- Score

183. How do you maintain endpoint protection solutions's Integrity?
<--- Score

184. Is there any reason to believe the opposite of my current belief?
<--- Score

185. Are you / should you be revolutionary or evolutionary?
<--- Score

186. In the past year, what have you done (or could you have done) to increase the accurate

perception of your company/brand as ethical and honest?

<--- Score

187. If you were responsible for initiating and implementing major changes in your organization, what steps might you take to ensure acceptance of those changes?

<--- Score

188. What are the success criteria that will indicate that endpoint protection solutions objectives have been met and the benefits delivered?

<--- Score

189. What are the barriers to increased endpoint protection solutions production?

<--- Score

190. Who is on the team?

<--- Score

191. What is the overall talent health of your organization as a whole at senior levels, and for each organization reporting to a member of the Senior Leadership Team?

<--- Score

192. If you got fired and a new hire took your place, what would she do different?

<--- Score

193. Is there a work around that you can use?

<--- Score

194. Have benefits been optimized with all key

stakeholders?
<--- Score

195. If there were zero limitations, what would you do differently?
<--- Score

196. Is your strategy driving your strategy? Or is the way in which you allocate resources driving your strategy?
<--- Score

197. Are you maintaining a past–present–future perspective throughout the endpoint protection solutions discussion?
<--- Score

198. Can you maintain your growth without detracting from the factors that have contributed to your success?
<--- Score

199. What role does communication play in the success or failure of a endpoint protection solutions project?
<--- Score

200. How do you go about securing endpoint protection solutions?
<--- Score

201. How do you proactively clarify deliverables and endpoint protection solutions quality expectations?
<--- Score

202. Why is endpoint protection solutions important

for you now?
<--- Score

203. How do you foster the skills, knowledge, talents, attributes, and characteristics you want to have?
<--- Score

204. What is the source of the strategies for endpoint protection solutions strengthening and reform?
<--- Score

205. What should you stop doing?
<--- Score

206. Is the endpoint protection solutions organization completing tasks effectively and efficiently?
<--- Score

207. Who do we want your customers to become?
<--- Score

208. Who are four people whose careers you have enhanced?
<--- Score

209. Ask yourself: how would you do this work if you only had one staff member to do it?
<--- Score

    Add up total points for this section:
    _ _ _ _ _ = Total points for this section

    Divided by: _ _ _ _ _ _ (number of
    statements answered) = _ _ _ _ _ _

Average score for this section

Transfer your score to the endpoint
protection solutions Index at the
beginning of the Self-Assessment.

Endpoint Protection Solutions and Managing Projects, Criteria for Project Managers:

1.0 Initiating Process Group: Endpoint Protection Solutions

1. Will the Endpoint Protection Solutions project meet the client requirements, and will it achieve the business success criteria that justified doing the Endpoint Protection Solutions project in the first place?

2. How should needs be met?

3. For technology Endpoint Protection Solutions projects only: Are all production support stakeholders (Business unit, technical support, & user) prepared for implementation with appropriate contingency plans?

4. First of all, should any action be taken?

5. How will you do it?

6. Which of six sigmas dmaic phases focuses on the measurement of internal process that affect factors that are critical to quality?

7. When will the Endpoint Protection Solutions project be done?

8. If action is called for, what form should it take?

9. Just how important is your work to the overall success of the Endpoint Protection Solutions project?

10. What technical work to do in each phase?

11. Are you certain deliverables are properly

completed and meet quality standards?

12. How well defined and documented were the Endpoint Protection Solutions project management processes you chose to use?

13. Do you know the roles & responsibilities required for this Endpoint Protection Solutions project?

14. Does the Endpoint Protection Solutions project team have enough people to execute the Endpoint Protection Solutions project plan?

15. During which stage of Risk planning are modeling techniques used to determine overall effects of risks on Endpoint Protection Solutions project objectives for high probability, high impact risks?

16. If the risk event occurs, what will you do?

17. Based on your Endpoint Protection Solutions project communication management plan, what worked well?

18. Although the Endpoint Protection Solutions project manager does not directly manage procurement and contracting activities, who does manage procurement and contracting activities in your organization then if not the PM?

19. How to control and approve each phase?

20. What must be done?

1.1 Project Charter: Endpoint Protection Solutions

21. What are the assigned resources?

22. Endpoint Protection Solutions project background: what is the primary motivation for this Endpoint Protection Solutions project?

23. How will you know a change is an improvement?

24. Why executive support?

25. Who are the stakeholders?

26. What is the business need?

27. Who ise input and support will this Endpoint Protection Solutions project require?

28. For whom?

29. Why have you chosen the aim you have set forth?

30. Why do you manage integration?

31. Did your Endpoint Protection Solutions project ask for this?

32. Where does all this information come from?

33. When will this occur?

34. How are Endpoint Protection Solutions projects different from operations?

35. Must Have?

36. What does it need to do?

37. Who manages integration?

38. Are there special technology requirements?

39. What is the most common tool for helping define the detail?

40. Why is it important?

1.2 Stakeholder Register: Endpoint Protection Solutions

41. Who wants to talk about Security?

42. How should employers make voices heard?

43. How much influence do they have on the Endpoint Protection Solutions project?

44. Is your organization ready for change?

45. What are the major Endpoint Protection Solutions project milestones requiring communications or providing communications opportunities?

46. What opportunities exist to provide communications?

47. How big is the gap?

48. What is the power of the stakeholder?

49. How will reports be created?

50. What & Why?

51. Who is managing stakeholder engagement?

1.3 Stakeholder Analysis Matrix: Endpoint Protection Solutions

52. Vital contracts and partners?

53. Cultural, attitudinal, behavioural?

54. Will the impacts be local, national or international?

55. Advantages of proposition?

56. What is the stakeholders power and status in relation to the Endpoint Protection Solutions project?

57. Guiding question: what is the issue at stake?

58. How are the threatened Endpoint Protection Solutions project targets being used?

59. What do you Evaluate?

60. What can the stakeholder prevent from happening?

61. Political effects?

62. Seasonality, weather effects?

63. Competitive advantages?

64. Global influences?

65. Who are potential allies and opponents?

66. Are the interests in line with the program objectives?

67. Competitors vulnerabilities?

68. If the baseline is now, and if its improved it will be better than now?

69. Partnership opportunities/synergies?

70. What is the range you need to look at?

2.0 Planning Process Group: Endpoint Protection Solutions

71. If a task is partitionable, is this a sufficient condition to reduce the Endpoint Protection Solutions project duration?

72. Is the identification of the problems, inequalities and gaps, with respective causes, clear in the Endpoint Protection Solutions project?

73. Product breakdown structure (pbs): what is the Endpoint Protection Solutions project result or product, and how should it look like, what are its parts?

74. Is the pace of implementing the products of the program ensuring the completeness of the results of the Endpoint Protection Solutions project?

75. What do you need to do?

76. Is the duration of the program sufficient to ensure a cycle that will Endpoint Protection Solutions project the sustainability of the interventions?

77. How do you integrate Endpoint Protection Solutions project Planning with the Iterative/ Evolutionary SDLC?

78. To what extent are the participating departments coordinating with each other?

79. Just how important is your work to the overall success of the Endpoint Protection Solutions project?

80. Explanation: is what the Endpoint Protection Solutions project intents to solve a hard question?

81. What is a Software Development Life Cycle (SDLC)?

82. You are creating your WBS and find that you keep decomposing tasks into smaller and smaller units. How can you tell when you are done?

83. Did you read it correctly?

84. Are the necessary foundations in place to ensure the sustainability of the results of the Endpoint Protection Solutions project?

85. How well will the chosen processes produce the expected results?

86. To what extent and in what ways are the Endpoint Protection Solutions project contributing to progress towards organizational reform?

87. What should you do next?

88. How will users learn how to use the deliverables?

89. What are the different approaches to building the WBS?

90. To what extent have public/private national resources and/or counterparts been mobilized to contribute to the programs objective and produce results and impacts?

2.1 Project Management Plan: Endpoint Protection Solutions

91. Is the appropriate plan selected based on your organizations objectives and evaluation criteria expressed in Principles and Guidelines policies?

92. What are the deliverables?

93. What are the known stakeholder requirements?

94. Did the planning effort collaborate to develop solutions that integrate expertise, policies, programs, and Endpoint Protection Solutions projects across entities?

95. What is the justification?

96. Why Change?

97. Are alternatives safe, functional, constructible, economical, reasonable and sustainable?

98. How well are you able to manage your risk?

99. How do you manage time?

100. What would you do differently?

101. Does the selected plan protect privacy?

102. Is the budget realistic?

103. Does the implementation plan have an appropriate division of responsibilities?

104. What went right?

105. What are the assumptions?

106. How do you manage integration?

107. When is the Endpoint Protection Solutions project management plan created?

108. What should you drop in order to add something new?

2.2 Scope Management Plan: Endpoint Protection Solutions

109. Has the Endpoint Protection Solutions project approach and development strategy of the Endpoint Protection Solutions project been defined, documented and accepted by the appropriate stakeholders?

110. Is the quality assurance team identified?

111. Is there an approved case?

112. Are funding resource estimates sufficiently detailed and documented for use in planning and tracking the Endpoint Protection Solutions project?

113. Are staffing resource estimates sufficiently detailed and documented for use in planning and tracking the Endpoint Protection Solutions project?

114. Has a quality assurance plan been developed for the Endpoint Protection Solutions project?

115. Is each item clearly and completely defined?

116. Are milestone deliverables effectively tracked and compared to Endpoint Protection Solutions project plan?

117. Is quality monitored from the perspective of the customers needs and expectations?

118. Is there a formal process for updating the Endpoint Protection Solutions project baseline?

119. Has your organization readiness assessment been conducted?

120. What if you do not have more detailed information on the report?

121. Are corrective actions taken when actual results are substantially different from detailed Endpoint Protection Solutions project plan (variances)?

122. Are written status reports provided on a designated frequent basis?

123. Have the personnel with the necessary skills and competence been identified and has agreement for participation in the Endpoint Protection Solutions project been reached with the appropriate management?

124. What threats might prevent you from getting there?

125. Have Endpoint Protection Solutions project team accountabilities & responsibilities been clearly defined?

126. Are staff skills known and available for each task?

127. Are vendor invoices audited for accuracy before payment?

2.3 Requirements Management Plan: Endpoint Protection Solutions

128. Who came up with this requirement?

129. What are you trying to do?

130. Why manage requirements?

131. Will you have access to stakeholders when you need them?

132. Do you understand the role that each stakeholder will play in the requirements process?

133. Are actual resource expenditures versus planned still acceptable?

134. Did you avoid subjective, flowery or non-specific statements?

135. Is the system software (non-operating system) new to the IT Endpoint Protection Solutions project team?

136. How will you communicate scheduled tasks to other team members?

137. Describe the process for rejecting the Endpoint Protection Solutions project requirements. Who has the authority to reject Endpoint Protection Solutions project requirements?

138. What performance metrics will be used?

139. Who will perform the analysis?

140. Is any organizational data being used or stored?

141. How do you know that you have done this right?

142. In case of software development; Should you have a test for each code module?

143. After the requirements are gathered and set forth on the requirements register, theyre little more than a laundry list of items. Some may be duplicates, some might conflict with others and some will be too broad or too vague to understand. Describe how the requirements will be analyzed. Who will perform the analysis?

144. Did you use declarative statements?

145. Is it new or replacing an existing business system or process?

146. Subject to change control?

147. Will you use an assessment of the Endpoint Protection Solutions project environment as a tool to discover risk to the requirements process?

2.4 Requirements Documentation: Endpoint Protection Solutions

148. Is your business case still valid?

149. Who provides requirements?

150. How will requirements be documented and who signs off on them?

151. Verifiability. can the requirements be checked?

152. What is your Elevator Speech?

153. Is the requirement realistically testable?

154. What will be the integration problems?

155. Where do you define what is a customer, what are the attributes of customer?

156. Are there legal issues?

157. Basic work/business process; high-level, what is being touched?

158. What are current process problems?

159. How to document system requirements?

160. What is effective documentation?

161. What are the acceptance criteria?

162. How much testing do you need to do to prove that your system is safe?

163. How do you know when a Requirement is accurate enough?

164. If applicable; are there issues linked with the fact that this is an offshore Endpoint Protection Solutions project?

165. What variations exist for a process?

166. Who is interacting with the system?

167. Where do system and software requirements come from, what are sources?

2.5 Requirements Traceability Matrix: Endpoint Protection Solutions

168. How will it affect the stakeholders personally in career?

169. Why use a WBS?

170. Why do you manage scope?

171. What percentage of Endpoint Protection Solutions projects are producing traceability matrices between requirements and other work products?

172. Describe the process for approving requirements so they can be added to the traceability matrix and Endpoint Protection Solutions project work can be performed. Will the Endpoint Protection Solutions project requirements become approved in writing?

173. How do you manage scope?

174. Will you use a Requirements Traceability Matrix?

175. Is there a requirements traceability process in place?

176. What is the WBS?

177. What are the chronologies, contingencies, consequences, criteria?

178. How small is small enough?

179. Do you have a clear understanding of all subcontracts in place?

2.6 Project Scope Statement: Endpoint Protection Solutions

180. Elements of scope management that deal with concept development ?

181. Is the scope of your Endpoint Protection Solutions project well defined?

182. What actions will be taken to mitigate the risk?

183. Will an issue form be in use?

184. Is the plan under configuration management?

185. Will the risk status be reported to management on a regular and frequent basis?

186. Identify how your team and you will create the Endpoint Protection Solutions project scope statement and the work breakdown structure (WBS). Document how you will create the Endpoint Protection Solutions project scope statement and WBS, and make sure you answer the following questions: In defining Endpoint Protection Solutions project scope and the WBS, will you and your Endpoint Protection Solutions project team be using methods defined by your organization, methods defined by the Endpoint Protection Solutions project management office (PMO), or other methods?

187. Change management vs. change leadership - what is the difference?

188. Is there a baseline plan against which to measure progress?

189. Is the Endpoint Protection Solutions project manager qualified and experienced in Endpoint Protection Solutions project management?

190. Has a method and process for requirement tracking been developed?

191. Will all tasks resulting from issues be entered into the Endpoint Protection Solutions project Plan and tracked through the plan?

192. What is a process you might recommend to verify the accuracy of the research deliverable?

193. Are there issues that could affect the existing requirements for the result, service, or product if the scope changes?

194. Were key Endpoint Protection Solutions project stakeholders brought into the Endpoint Protection Solutions project Plan?

195. How often will scope changes be reviewed?

196. Will statistics related to QA be collected, trends analyzed, and problems raised as issues?

197. Will tasks be marked complete only after QA has been successfully completed?

2.7 Assumption and Constraint Log: Endpoint Protection Solutions

198. Does the system design reflect the requirements?

199. When can log be discarded?

200. Are there procedures in place to effectively manage interdependencies with other Endpoint Protection Solutions projects / systems?

201. Are funding and staffing resource estimates sufficiently detailed and documented for use in planning and tracking the Endpoint Protection Solutions project?

202. Does the traceability documentation describe the tool and/or mechanism to be used to capture traceability throughout the life cycle?

203. Is the process working, and people are not executing in compliance of the process?

204. What is positive about the current process?

205. Are there cosmetic errors that hinder readability and comprehension?

206. Security analysis has access to information that is sanitized?

207. What do you audit?

208. What strengths do you have?

209. Is there documentation of system capability requirements, data requirements, environment requirements, security requirements, and computer and hardware requirements?

210. If appropriate, is the deliverable content consistent with current Endpoint Protection Solutions project documents and in compliance with the Document Management Plan?

211. Are there processes defining how software will be developed including development methods, overall timeline for development, software product standards, and traceability?

212. What would you gain if you spent time working to improve this process?

213. Have all stakeholders been identified?

214. What other teams / processes would be impacted by changes to the current process, and how?

215. What does an audit system look like?

216. Are there ways to reduce the time it takes to get something approved?

217. Is this process still needed?

2.8 Work Breakdown Structure: Endpoint Protection Solutions

218. Do you need another level?

219. Why would you develop a Work Breakdown Structure?

220. When does it have to be done?

221. Is the work breakdown structure (wbs) defined and is the scope of the Endpoint Protection Solutions project clear with assigned deliverable owners?

222. Where does it take place?

223. How will you and your Endpoint Protection Solutions project team define the Endpoint Protection Solutions projects scope and work breakdown structure?

224. Who has to do it?

225. How far down?

226. How many levels?

227. What is the probability that the Endpoint Protection Solutions project duration will exceed xx weeks?

228. Can you make it?

229. Is it still viable?

230. How big is a work-package?

231. What is the probability of completing the Endpoint Protection Solutions project in less that xx days?

232. When do you stop?

233. How much detail?

234. What has to be done?

235. Is it a change in scope?

2.9 WBS Dictionary: Endpoint Protection Solutions

236. What is the end result of a work package?

237. Are direct or indirect cost adjustments being accomplished according to accounting procedures acceptable to us?

238. Are the contractors estimates of costs at completion reconcilable with cost data reported to us?

239. Where learning is used in developing underlying budgets is there a direct relationship between anticipated learning and time phased budgets?

240. Are indirect costs accumulated for comparison with the corresponding budgets?

241. Are material costs reported within the same period as that in which BCWP is earned for that material?

242. Do the lines of authority for incurring indirect costs correspond to the lines of responsibility for management control of the same components of costs?

243. The anticipated business volume?

244. What are you counting on?

245. Cwbs elements to be subcontracted, with identification of subcontractors?

246. Are data being used by managers in an effective manner to ascertain Endpoint Protection Solutions project or functional status, to identify reasons or significant variance, and to initiate appropriate corrective action?

247. Identify potential or actual overruns and underruns?

248. Changes in the current direct and Endpoint Protection Solutions projected base?

249. Is future work which cannot be planned in detail subdivided to the extent practicable for budgeting and scheduling purposes?

250. What went wrong?

251. Is work progressively subdivided into detailed work packages as requirements are defined?

252. Knowledgeable Endpoint Protection Solutions projections of future performance?

253. Does the contractors system provide for determination of price variance by comparing planned Vs actual commitments?

254. Is work properly classified as measured effort, LOE, or apportioned effort and appropriately separated?

255. All cwbs elements specified for external

reporting?

2.10 Schedule Management Plan: Endpoint Protection Solutions

256. Is there a Steering Committee in place?

257. What is the estimated time to complete the Endpoint Protection Solutions project if status quo is maintained?

258. Are changes in deliverable commitments agreed to by all affected groups & individuals?

259. Has the scope management document been updated and distributed to help prevent scope creep?

260. Have activity relationships and interdependencies within tasks been adequately identified?

261. Does the Endpoint Protection Solutions project have quality set of schedule BOEs?

262. Are the results of quality assurance reviews provided to affected groups & individuals?

263. Are there any activities or deliverables being added or gold-plated that could be dropped or scaled back without falling short of the original requirement?

264. Endpoint Protection Solutions project definition & scope?

265. Does all Endpoint Protection Solutions project

documentation reside in a common repository for easy access?

266. Are assumptions being identified, recorded, analyzed, qualified and closed?

267. Is Endpoint Protection Solutions project status reviewed with the steering and executive teams at appropriate intervals?

268. Are scheduled deliverables actually delivered?

269. Have all unresolved risks been documented?

270. Have Endpoint Protection Solutions project management standards and procedures been identified / established and documented?

271. What will be the final cost of the Endpoint Protection Solutions project if status quo is maintained?

272. Have the key functions and capabilities been defined and assigned to each release or iteration?

273. Is the communication plan being followed?

274. Are the people assigned to the Endpoint Protection Solutions project sufficiently qualified?

2.11 Activity List: Endpoint Protection Solutions

275. The wbs is developed as part of a joint planning session. and how do you know that youhave done this right?

276. Should you include sub-activities?

277. What will be performed?

278. How detailed should a Endpoint Protection Solutions project get?

279. How much slack is available in the Endpoint Protection Solutions project?

280. Are the required resources available or need to be acquired?

281. What is your organizations history in doing similar activities?

282. How will it be performed?

283. How do you determine the late start (LS) for each activity?

284. What is the probability the Endpoint Protection Solutions project can be completed in xx weeks?

285. What is the LF and LS for each activity?

286. For other activities, how much delay can be tolerated?

287. Is there anything planned that does not need to be here?

288. How can the Endpoint Protection Solutions project be displayed graphically to better visualize the activities?

289. What are the critical bottleneck activities?

290. Can you determine the activity that must finish, before this activity can start?

291. When do the individual activities need to start and finish?

292. In what sequence?

2.12 Activity Attributes: Endpoint Protection Solutions

293. What conclusions/generalizations can you draw from this?

294. Is there a trend during the year?

295. Resource is assigned to?

296. Does your organization of the data change its meaning?

297. How difficult will it be to complete specific activities on this Endpoint Protection Solutions project?

298. How much activity detail is required?

299. What is the general pattern here?

300. Can you re-assign any activities to another resource to resolve an over-allocation?

301. What is missing?

302. Has management defined a definite timeframe for the turnaround or Endpoint Protection Solutions project window?

303. Would you consider either of corresponding activities an outlier?

304. Activity: what is Missing?

305. Which method produces the more accurate cost assignment?

306. Activity: fair or not fair?

307. How difficult will it be to do specific activities on this Endpoint Protection Solutions project?

308. What activity do you think you should spend the most time on?

309. Resources to accomplish the work?

310. Can more resources be added?

2.13 Milestone List: Endpoint Protection Solutions

311. Usps (unique selling points)?

312. Describe the concept of the technology, product or service that will be or has been developed. How will it be used?

313. Continuity, supply chain robustness?

314. Legislative effects?

315. Identify critical paths (one or more) and which activities are on the critical path?

316. Insurmountable weaknesses?

317. Describe your organizations strengths and core competencies. What factors will make your organization succeed?

318. How will you get the word out to customers?

319. Sustainable financial backing?

320. What has been done so far?

321. Own known vulnerabilities?

322. How late can the activity finish?

323. How difficult will it be to do specific activities on

this Endpoint Protection Solutions project?

324. New USPs?

325. What background experience, skills, and strengths does the team bring to your organization?

326. How soon can the activity finish?

327. How late can each activity be finished and started?

328. Timescales, deadlines and pressures?

2.14 Network Diagram: Endpoint Protection Solutions

329. How confident can you be in your milestone dates and the delivery date?

330. What job or jobs precede it?

331. What controls the start and finish of a job?

332. What are the Key Success Factors?

333. Which type of network diagram allows you to depict four types of dependencies?

334. What activity must be completed immediately before this activity can start?

335. What must be completed before an activity can be started?

336. How difficult will it be to do specific activities on this Endpoint Protection Solutions project?

337. What are the tools?

338. If the Endpoint Protection Solutions project network diagram cannot change and you have extra personnel resources, what is the BEST thing to do?

339. If x is long, what would be the completion time if you break x into two parallel parts of y weeks and z weeks?

340. Will crashing x weeks return more in benefits than it costs?

341. Are you on time?

342. What are the Major Administrative Issues?

343. Are the gantt chart and/or network diagram updated periodically and used to assess the overall Endpoint Protection Solutions project timetable?

344. Planning: who, how long, what to do?

345. Are the required resources available?

346. Can you calculate the confidence level?

347. Exercise: what is the probability that the Endpoint Protection Solutions project duration will exceed xx weeks?

348. What can be done concurrently?

2.15 Activity Resource Requirements: Endpoint Protection Solutions

349. Which logical relationship does the PDM use most often?

350. What is the Work Plan Standard?

351. Time for overtime?

352. Why do you do that?

353. Are there unresolved issues that need to be addressed?

354. How many signatures do you require on a check and does this match what is in your policy and procedures?

355. Other support in specific areas?

356. When does monitoring begin?

357. Anything else?

358. Organizational Applicability?

359. Do you use tools like decomposition and rolling-wave planning to produce the activity list and other outputs?

360. How do you handle petty cash?

361. What are constraints that you might find during the Human Resource Planning process?

2.16 Resource Breakdown Structure: Endpoint Protection Solutions

362. Which resource planning tool provides information on resource responsibility and accountability?

363. Who will use the system?

364. Why do you do it?

365. The list could probably go on, but, the thing that you would most like to know is, How long & How much?

366. Who is allowed to see what data about which resources?

367. How difficult will it be to do specific activities on this Endpoint Protection Solutions project?

368. What is each stakeholders desired outcome for the Endpoint Protection Solutions project?

369. Goals for the Endpoint Protection Solutions project. What is each stakeholders desired outcome for the Endpoint Protection Solutions project?

370. When do they need the information?

371. Why time management?

372. How should the information be delivered?

373. What is Endpoint Protection Solutions project communication management?

374. What can you do to improve productivity?

375. What is the primary purpose of the human resource plan?

376. Changes based on input from stakeholders?

2.17 Activity Duration Estimates: Endpoint Protection Solutions

377. Are performance reviews conducted regularly to assess the status of Endpoint Protection Solutions projects?

378. Are team building activities completed to improve team performance?

379. Account for the four frames of organizations. How can they help Endpoint Protection Solutions project managers understand your organizational context for Endpoint Protection Solutions projects?

380. What are the main types of goods and services being outsourced?

381. Are many products available?

382. What are two suggestions for ensuring adequate change control on Endpoint Protection Solutions projects that involve outside contracts?

383. Which is the BEST Endpoint Protection Solutions project management tool to use to determine the longest time the Endpoint Protection Solutions project will take?

384. How do you enter durations, link tasks, and view critical path information?

385. What are some crucial elements of a good

Endpoint Protection Solutions project plan?

386. Briefly summarize the work done by Maslow, Herzberg, McClellan, McGregor, Ouchi, Thamhain and Wilemon, and Covey. How do theories relate to Endpoint Protection Solutions project management?

387. How does Endpoint Protection Solutions project management relate to other disciplines?

388. Are changes to the scope managed according to defined procedures?

389. After changes are approved are Endpoint Protection Solutions project documents updated and distributed?

390. How difficult will it be to do specific activities on this Endpoint Protection Solutions project?

391. Endpoint Protection Solutions project manager has received activity duration estimates from his team. Which does one need in order to complete schedule development?

392. What is the difference between % Complete and % work?

393. How difficult will it be to complete specific activities on this Endpoint Protection Solutions project?

394. Do an internet search on earning pmp certification. be sure to search for yahoo groups related to this topic. what are the options you found to help people prepare for the exam?

395. Are risks monitored to determine if an event has occurred or if the mitigation was successful?

2.18 Duration Estimating Worksheet: Endpoint Protection Solutions

396. Is the Endpoint Protection Solutions project responsive to community need?

397. Why estimate costs?

398. How should ongoing costs be monitored to try to keep the Endpoint Protection Solutions project within budget?

399. What is next?

400. Science = process: remember the scientific method?

401. How can the Endpoint Protection Solutions project be displayed graphically to better visualize the activities?

402. What is an Average Endpoint Protection Solutions project?

403. Value pocket identification & quantification what are value pockets?

404. What is the total time required to complete the Endpoint Protection Solutions project if no delays occur?

405. Why estimate time and cost?

406. What questions do you have?

407. What info is needed?

408. Do any colleagues have experience with your organization and/or RFPs?

409. Is a construction detail attached (to aid in explanation)?

410. Is this operation cost effective?

411. What is cost and Endpoint Protection Solutions project cost management?

412. What is your role?

2.19 Project Schedule: Endpoint Protection Solutions

413. To what degree is do you feel the entire team was committed to the Endpoint Protection Solutions project schedule?

414. How can slack be negative?

415. What does that mean?

416. How can you shorten the schedule?

417. Month Endpoint Protection Solutions project take?

418. Master Endpoint Protection Solutions project schedule?

419. Have all Endpoint Protection Solutions project delays been adequately accounted for, communicated to all stakeholders and adjustments made in overall Endpoint Protection Solutions project schedule?

420. How detailed should a Endpoint Protection Solutions project get?

421. Activity charts and bar charts are graphical representations of a Endpoint Protection Solutions project schedule ...how do they differ?

422. Your best shot for providing estimations how complex/how much work does the activity require?

423. What is the most mis-scheduled part of process?

424. Is infrastructure setup part of your Endpoint Protection Solutions project?

425. Why is software Endpoint Protection Solutions project disaster so common?

426. What is the purpose of a Endpoint Protection Solutions project schedule?

427. Why is this particularly bad?

428. Did the final product meet or exceed user expectations?

429. Eliminate unnecessary activities. Are there activities that came from a template or previous Endpoint Protection Solutions project that are not applicable on this phase of this Endpoint Protection Solutions project?

2.20 Cost Management Plan: Endpoint Protection Solutions

430. Are any non-compliance issues that exist due to State practices communicated to your organization?

431. How does the proposed individual meet each requirement?

432. Is there an onboarding process in place?

433. Have the key elements of a coherent Endpoint Protection Solutions project management strategy been established?

434. Resources – how will human resources be scheduled during each phase of the Endpoint Protection Solutions project?

435. What would you do differently what did not work?

436. Quality assurance overheads?

437. Are schedule deliverables actually delivered?

438. Are risk triggers captured?

439. Are all key components of a Quality Assurance Plan present?

440. Are the quality tools and methods identified in the Quality Plan appropriate to the Endpoint

Protection Solutions project?

441. Milestones – what are the key dates in executing the contract plan?

442. Has a Endpoint Protection Solutions project Communications Plan been developed?

443. Forecasts – how will the cost to complete the Endpoint Protection Solutions project be forecast?

444. What does this mean to a cost or scheduler manager?

445. Is stakeholder involvement adequate?

2.21 Activity Cost Estimates: Endpoint Protection Solutions

446. Is there anything unique in this Endpoint Protection Solutions projects scope statement that will affect resources?

447. What is the activity inventory?

448. Can you change your activities?

449. Review – what are some common errors in activities to avoid?

450. Is costing method consistent with study goals?

451. What do you want to know about the stay to know if costs were inappropriately high or low?

452. Can you delete activities or make them inactive?

453. Scope statement only direct or indirect costs as well?

454. When do you enter into PPM?

455. Who determines the quality and expertise of contractors?

456. Were the costs or charges reasonable?

457. How do you fund change orders?

458. What are the audit requirements?

459. What is the last item a Endpoint Protection Solutions project manager must do to finalize Endpoint Protection Solutions project close-out?

460. Were sponsors and decision makers available when needed outside regularly scheduled meetings?

461. Was the consultant knowledgeable about the program?

462. What is Endpoint Protection Solutions project cost management?

463. Are cost subtotals needed?

464. Does the estimator estimate by task or by person?

465. Based on your Endpoint Protection Solutions project communication management plan, what worked well?

2.22 Cost Estimating Worksheet: Endpoint Protection Solutions

466. What is the purpose of estimating?

467. Who is best positioned to know and assist in identifying corresponding factors?

468. What is the estimated labor cost today based upon this information?

469. Is it feasible to establish a control group arrangement?

470. Does the Endpoint Protection Solutions project provide innovative ways for stakeholders to overcome obstacles or deliver better outcomes?

471. Will the Endpoint Protection Solutions project collaborate with the local community and leverage resources?

472. What costs are to be estimated?

473. How will the results be shared and to whom?

474. Is the Endpoint Protection Solutions project responsive to community need?

475. What will others want?

476. Ask: are others positioned to know, are others credible, and will others cooperate?

477. What additional Endpoint Protection Solutions project(s) could be initiated as a result of this Endpoint Protection Solutions project?

478. What can be included?

479. What happens to any remaining funds not used?

480. Identify the timeframe necessary to monitor progress and collect data to determine how the selected measure has changed?

481. Can a trend be established from historical performance data on the selected measure and are the criteria for using trend analysis or forecasting methods met?

2.23 Cost Baseline: Endpoint Protection Solutions

482. What does a good WBS NOT look like?

483. Endpoint Protection Solutions project goals -should others be reconsidered?

484. What would the life cycle costs be?

485. Have all approved changes to the schedule baseline been identified and impact on the Endpoint Protection Solutions project documented?

486. Has the actual cost of the Endpoint Protection Solutions project (or Endpoint Protection Solutions project phase) been tallied and compared to the approved budget?

487. How difficult will it be to do specific tasks on the Endpoint Protection Solutions project?

488. Pcs for your new business. what would the life cycle costs be?

489. If you sold 10x widgets on a day, what would the affect on profits be?

490. Is there anything unique in this Endpoint Protection Solutions projects scope statement that will affect resources?

491. Escalation criteria met?

492. How do you manage cost?

493. Has the Endpoint Protection Solutions project documentation been archived or otherwise disposed as described in the Endpoint Protection Solutions project communication plan?

494. Have the lessons learned been filed with the Endpoint Protection Solutions project Management Office?

495. Where do changes come from?

496. Is the cr within Endpoint Protection Solutions project scope?

497. Why do you manage cost?

498. For what purpose ?

2.24 Quality Management Plan: Endpoint Protection Solutions

499. Does a documented Endpoint Protection Solutions project organizational policy & plan (i.e. governance model) exist?

500. Who is responsible for writing the qapp?

501. Are there unnecessary steps that are creating bottlenecks and/or causing people to wait?

502. Have all involved stakeholders and work groups committed to the Endpoint Protection Solutions project?

503. Are you following the quality standards?

504. What is quality and how will you ensure it?

505. How is staff trained on the recording of field notes?

506. How do you prioritize?

507. Documented results available?

508. How many Endpoint Protection Solutions project staff does this specific process affect?

509. What are you trying to accomplish?

510. How does your organization manage work to

promote cooperation, individual initiative, innovation, flexibility, communications, and knowledge/skill sharing across work units?

511. How are changes recorded?

512. What are your organizations key processes (product, service, business, and support)?

513. With the five whys method, the team considers why the issue being explored occurred. do others then take that initial answer and ask why?

514. Is the amount of effort justified by the anticipated value of forming a new process?

515. What are your key performance measures/ indicators for tracking progress relative to your action plans?

516. Who gets results of work?

517. How do senior leaders create an environment that encourages learning and innovation?

2.25 Quality Metrics: Endpoint Protection Solutions

518. What is the benchmark?

519. Has risk analysis been adequately reviewed?

520. Is the reporting frequency appropriate?

521. Do the operators focus on determining; is there anything you need to worry about?

522. Filter visualizations of interest?

523. Are applicable standards referenced and available?

524. How is it being measured?

525. How should customers provide input?

526. What metrics are important and most beneficial to measure?

527. Are quality metrics defined?

528. How do you know if everyone is trying to improve the right things?

529. What level of statistical confidence do you use?

530. Where is quality now?

531. Can visual measures help you to filter visualizations of interest?

532. How are requirements conflicts resolved?

533. What documentation is required?

534. What if the biggest risk to your business were the already stated people who do not complain?

535. Was review conducted per standard protocols?

2.26 Process Improvement Plan: Endpoint Protection Solutions

536. If a process improvement framework is being used, which elements will help the problems and goals listed?

537. Where do you focus?

538. Why quality management?

539. Have storage and access mechanisms and procedures been determined?

540. Modeling current processes is great, and will you ever see a return on that investment?

541. Why do you want to achieve the goal?

542. What lessons have you learned so far?

543. What personnel are the change agents for your initiative?

544. Does your process ensure quality?

545. What actions are needed to address the problems and achieve the goals?

546. Who should prepare the process improvement action plan?

547. Are you meeting the quality standards?

548. Are there forms and procedures to collect and record the data?

549. Where do you want to be?

550. What personnel are the coaches for your initiative?

551. How do you manage quality?

552. Everyone agrees on what process improvement is, right?

553. Management commitment at all levels?

554. Has a process guide to collect the data been developed?

555. Purpose of goal: the motive is determined by asking, why do you want to achieve this goal?

2.27 Responsibility Assignment Matrix: Endpoint Protection Solutions

556. Does each role with Accountable responsibility have the authority within your organization to make the required decisions?

557. Does the contractors system provide unit or lot costs when applicable?

558. Are estimates of costs at completion generated in a rational, consistent manner?

559. Too many is: do all the identified roles need to be routinely informed or only in exceptional circumstances?

560. Budgeted cost for work scheduled?

561. Are work packages assigned to performing organizations?

562. Authorization to proceed with all authorized work?

563. Who is responsible for work and budgets for each wbs?

564. When performing is split among two or more roles, is the work clearly defined so that the efforts are coordinated and the communication is clear?

565. Does the contractors system identify work

accomplishment against the schedule plan?

566. Are your organizations and items of cost assigned to each pool identified?

567. What cost control tool do many experts say is crucial to Endpoint Protection Solutions project management?

568. Endpoint Protection Solutions projected economic escalation?

569. Are authorized changes being incorporated in a timely manner?

570. Most people let you know when others re too busy, and are others really too busy?

571. Are data elements reconcilable between internal summary reports and reports forwarded to stakeholders?

572. Who is the sponsor?

573. What travel needed?

574. Is data disseminated to the contractors management timely, accurate, and usable?

2.28 Roles and Responsibilities: Endpoint Protection Solutions

575. Implementation of actions: Who are the responsible units?

576. What specific behaviors did you observe?

577. What are your major roles and responsibilities in the area of performance measurement and assessment?

578. What is working well?

579. What should you do now to ensure that you are exceeding expectations and excelling in your current position?

580. Does your vision/mission support a culture of quality data?

581. What should you highlight for improvement?

582. Are the quality assurance functions and related roles and responsibilities clearly defined?

583. What areas of supervision are challenging for you?

584. What should you do now to prepare for your career 5+ years from now?

585. Are your budgets supportive of a culture of

quality data?

586. Attainable / achievable: the goal is attainable; can you actually accomplish the goal?

587. Be specific; avoid generalities. Thank you and great work alone are insufficient. What exactly do you appreciate and why?

588. Who is involved?

589. What expectations were met?

590. Authority: what areas/Endpoint Protection Solutions projects in your work do you have the authority to decide upon and act on the already stated decisions?

591. Do the values and practices inherent in the culture of your organization foster or hinder the process?

592. What should you do now to ensure that you are meeting all expectations of your current position?

593. Is feedback clearly communicated and non-judgmental?

2.29 Human Resource Management Plan: Endpoint Protection Solutions

594. How are superior performers differentiated from average performers?

595. Does the Endpoint Protection Solutions project have a Quality Culture?

596. Do Endpoint Protection Solutions project managers participating in the Endpoint Protection Solutions project know the Endpoint Protection Solutions projects true status first hand?

597. Are estimating assumptions and constraints captured?

598. Has the Endpoint Protection Solutions project scope been baselined?

599. Who needs training?

600. Alignment to strategic goals & objectives?

601. Are non-critical path items updated and agreed upon with the teams?

602. Are changes in scope (deliverable commitments) agreed to by all affected groups & individuals?

603. Is your organization certified as a supplier, wholesaler, regular dealer, or manufacturer of corresponding products/supplies?

604. Has a provision been made to reassess Endpoint Protection Solutions project risks at various Endpoint Protection Solutions project stages?

605. Have all involved Endpoint Protection Solutions project stakeholders and work groups committed to the Endpoint Protection Solutions project?

606. Account for the purpose of this Endpoint Protection Solutions project by describing, at a high-level, what will be done. What is this Endpoint Protection Solutions project aiming to achieve?

607. What did you have to assume to be true to complete the charter?

608. Were stakeholders aware and supportive of the principles and practices of modern cost estimation?

609. Specific - is the objective clear in terms of what, how, when, and where the situation will be changed?

610. Are there dependencies with other initiatives or Endpoint Protection Solutions projects?

2.30 Communications Management Plan: Endpoint Protection Solutions

611. Who will use or be affected by the result of a Endpoint Protection Solutions project?

612. How do you manage communications?

613. Do you feel more overwhelmed by stakeholders?

614. What data is going to be required?

615. What is the stakeholders level of authority?

616. Will messages be directly related to the release strategy or phases of the Endpoint Protection Solutions project?

617. Is the stakeholder role recognized by your organization?

618. What are the interrelationships?

619. Timing: when do the effects of the communication take place?

620. How were corresponding initiatives successful?

621. Are stakeholders internal or external?

622. Why is stakeholder engagement important?

623. Do you then often overlook a key stakeholder or

stakeholder group?

624. How did the term stakeholder originate?

625. What steps can you take for a positive relationship?

626. Who have you worked with in past, similar initiatives?

627. Do you prepare stakeholder engagement plans?

628. Are others needed?

629. What does the stakeholder need from the team?

2.31 Risk Management Plan: Endpoint Protection Solutions

630. Why do you want risk management?

631. What worked well?

632. Has something like this been done before?

633. What are the cost, schedule and resource impacts if the risk does occur?

634. What things might go wrong?

635. How is risk monitoring performed?

636. Do you have a mechanism for managing change?

637. Are tool mentors available?

638. How is the audit profession changing?

639. Is the customer technically sophisticated in the product area?

640. Is there anything you would now do differently on your Endpoint Protection Solutions project based on this experience?

641. What will drive change?

642. Is the customer willing to commit significant time to the requirements gathering process?

643. Are there new risks that mitigation strategies might introduce?

644. Are status updates being made on schedule and are the updates clearly described?

645. Costs associated with late delivery or a defective product?

646. Are requirements fully understood by the software engineering team and customers?

647. Can the Endpoint Protection Solutions project proceed without assuming the risk?

648. What risks are tracked?

649. How are risk analvsis and prioritization performed?

2.32 Risk Register: Endpoint Protection Solutions

650. Recovery actions - planned actions taken once a risk has occurred to allow you to move on. What should you do after?

651. What is the probability and impact of the risk occurring?

652. What action, if any, has been taken to respond to the risk?

653. Having taken action, how did the responses effect change, and where is the Endpoint Protection Solutions project now?

654. Are corrective measures implemented as planned?

655. Schedule impact/severity estimated range (workdays) assume the event happens, what is the potential impact?

656. Manageability – have mitigations to the risk been identified?

657. How could corresponding Risk affect the Endpoint Protection Solutions project in terms of cost and schedule?

658. Assume the event happens, what is the Most Likely impact?

659. What may happen or not go according to plan?

660. What would the impact to the Endpoint Protection Solutions project objectives be should the risk arise?

661. Risk documentation: what reporting formats and processes will be used for risk management activities?

662. What has changed since the last period?

663. Who needs to know about this?

664. What should you do when?

665. Who is accountable?

666. How are risks graded?

667. Amongst the action plans and recommendations that you have to introduce are there some that could stop or delay the overall program?

668. What are the major risks facing the Endpoint Protection Solutions project?

669. Assume the risk event or situation happens, what would the impact be?

2.33 Probability and Impact Assessment: Endpoint Protection Solutions

670. What are the current requirements of the customer?

671. What is the probability of the risk occurring?

672. Monitoring of the overall Endpoint Protection Solutions project status – are there any changes in the Endpoint Protection Solutions project that can effect and cause new possible risks?

673. Do the people have the right combinations of skills?

674. What should be the requirement of organizational restructuring as each subEndpoint Protection Solutions project goes through a different lifecycle phase?

675. Can you avoid altogether some things that might go wrong?

676. Which risks need to move on to Perform Quantitative Risk Analysis?

677. How will economic events and trends likely affect the Endpoint Protection Solutions project?

678. What are the probabilities of chosen technologies being suitable for local conditions?

679. Do requirements put excessive performance constraints on the product?

680. Can this technology be absorbed with current level of expertise available in your organization?

681. Why has this particular mode of contracting been chosen?

682. What are the uncertainties associated with the technology selected for the Endpoint Protection Solutions project?

683. Have decisions that should be left open because of inadequate information on technology been identified and responsibility assigned for reducing the uncertainty?

684. Have staff received necessary training?

685. How completely has the customer been identified?

686. Have you ascribed a level of confidence to every critical technical objective?

687. Anticipated volatility of the requirements?

2.34 Probability and Impact Matrix: Endpoint Protection Solutions

688. Are testing tools available and suitable?

689. What are ways to measure and evaluate risks?

690. How to prioritize risks?

691. Mitigation -how can you avoid the risk?

692. What are the chances the risk events will occur?

693. Does the customer understand the software process?

694. How well is the risk understood?

695. Premium on reliability of product?

696. Who is going to be the consortium leader?

697. Are formal technical reviews part of this process?

698. Which is an input to the risk management process?

699. What are the methods to deal with risks?

700. What can you use the analyzed risks for?

701. What are the likely future requirements?

702. Do you train all developers in the process?

703. Who should be notified of the occurrence of each of the risk indicators?

704. Can you handle the investment risk?

705. Do you know the order of planning yet?

2.35 Risk Data Sheet: Endpoint Protection Solutions

706. How can it happen?

707. Are new hazards created?

708. Whom do you serve (customers)?

709. What if client refuses?

710. What is the chance that it will happen?

711. What will be the consequences if the risk happens?

712. What actions can be taken to eliminate or remove risk?

713. Potential for recurrence?

714. How reliable is the data source?

715. What was measured?

716. Type of risk identified?

717. What is the likelihood of it happening?

718. What are you trying to achieve (Objectives)?

719. What are your core values?

720. Is the data sufficiently specified in terms of the type of failure being analyzed, and its frequency or probability?

721. Has the most cost-effective solution been chosen?

722. Risk of what?

723. What were the Causes that contributed?

724. What are the main opportunities available to you that you should grab while you can?

725. If it happens, what are the consequences?

2.36 Procurement Management Plan: Endpoint Protection Solutions

726. Is documentation created for communication with the suppliers and Vendors?

727. Published materials?

728. Was the Endpoint Protection Solutions project schedule reviewed by all stakeholders and formally accepted?

729. Are tasks tracked by hours?

730. Have the key elements of a coherent Endpoint Protection Solutions project management strategy been established?

731. What were things that you did very well and want to do the same again on the next Endpoint Protection Solutions project?

732. If independent estimates will be needed as evaluation criteria, who will prepare them and when?

733. Are internal Endpoint Protection Solutions project status meetings held at reasonable intervals?

734. Have key stakeholders been identified?

735. Was the scope definition used in task sequencing?

736. Are cause and effect determined for risks when others occur?

737. Are any non-compliance issues that exist communicated to your organization?

738. Are updated Endpoint Protection Solutions project time & resource estimates reasonable based on the current Endpoint Protection Solutions project stage?

739. Public engagement – did you get it right?

740. How and when do you enter into Endpoint Protection Solutions project Procurement Management?

741. Is there a formal set of procedures supporting Issues Management?

742. How will multiple providers be managed?

2.37 Source Selection Criteria: Endpoint Protection Solutions

743. With the rapid changes in information technology, will media be readable in five or ten years?

744. What are the most critical evaluation criteria that prove to be tiebreakers in the evaluation of proposals?

745. How much past performance information should be requested?

746. Does your documentation identify why the team concurs or differs with reported performance from past performance report (CPARs, questionnaire responses, etc.)?

747. What is the basis of an estimate and what assumptions were made?

748. Does an evaluation need to include the identification of strengths and weaknesses?

749. Is the contracting office likely to receive more purchase requests for this item or service during the coming year?

750. Are there any specific considerations that precludes offers from being selected as the awardee?

751. What aspects should the contracting officer brief the Endpoint Protection Solutions project on prior to

evaluation of proposals?

752. How should comments received in response to a RFP be handled?

753. What are open book debriefings?

754. What are the steps in performing a cost/tech tradeoff?

755. How should oral presentations be prepared for?

756. Can you reasonably estimate total organization requirements for the coming year?

757. Is a letter of commitment from each proposed team member and key subcontractor included?

758. Can you prevent comparison of proposals?

759. What management structure does your organization consider as optimal for performing the contract?

760. What are the most common types of rating systems?

761. What past performance information should be requested?

762. What can not be disclosed?

2.38 Stakeholder Management Plan: Endpoint Protection Solutions

763. Does the plan conform to standards?

764. Does the business case include how the Endpoint Protection Solutions project aligns with your organizations strategic goals & objectives?

765. How are you doing/what can be done better?

766. Has a capability assessment been conducted?

767. Are the payment terms being followed?

768. Have all team members been part of identifying risks?

769. What is the primary function of the Activity Decomposition Decision Tree?

770. Will all relevant stakeholders be included within the review process?

771. Where to get additional help?

772. Is there any form of automated support for Issues Management?

773. Are there standards for code development?

774. Who is responsible for arranging and managing the review(s)?

775. Is there a set of procedures defining the scope, procedures, and deliverables defining quality control?

776. Were Endpoint Protection Solutions project team members involved in detailed estimating and scheduling?

777. Which impacts could serve as impediments?

2.39 Change Management Plan: Endpoint Protection Solutions

778. Is there a software application relevant to this deliverable?

779. What new behaviours are required?

780. What are you trying to achieve as a result of communication?

781. What are the essentials of the message?

782. Does this change represent a completely new process for your organization, or a different application of an existing process?

783. What are the responsibilities assigned to each role?

784. Identify the current level of skills and knowledge and behaviours of the group that will be impacted on. What prerequisite knowledge do corresponding groups need?

785. What did the people around you say about it?

786. How does the principle of senders and receivers make the Endpoint Protection Solutions project communications effort more complex?

787. Will a different work structure focus people on what is important?

788. When developing your communication plan do you address : When should the given message be communicated?

789. Has the target training audience been identified and nominated?

790. Will the culture embrace or reject this change?

791. What is the worst thing that can happen if you communicate information?

792. Has the training provider been established?

793. Where will the funds come from?

794. What are the specific target groups / audience that will be impacted by this change?

795. Is there support for this application(s) and are the details available for distribution?

3.0 Executing Process Group: Endpoint Protection Solutions

796. What are the typical Endpoint Protection Solutions project management skills?

797. It under budget or over budget?

798. Will a new application be developed using existing hardware, software, and networks?

799. What are the main processes included in Endpoint Protection Solutions project quality management?

800. Do the products created live up to the necessary quality?

801. Will new hardware or software be required for servers or client machines?

802. What are the Endpoint Protection Solutions project management deliverables of each process group?

803. What are the main types of contracts if you do decide to outsource?

804. What are deliverables of your Endpoint Protection Solutions project?

805. How can your organization use a weighted decision matrix to evaluate proposals as part of

source selection?

806. Mitigate. what will you do to minimize the impact should a risk event occur?

807. How could you control progress of your Endpoint Protection Solutions project?

808. What were things that you did well, and could improve, and how?

809. How does Endpoint Protection Solutions project management relate to other disciplines?

810. Does the Endpoint Protection Solutions project team have the right skills?

811. Why is it important to determine activity sequencing on Endpoint Protection Solutions projects?

812. How many different communication channels does the Endpoint Protection Solutions project team have?

813. What are crucial elements of successful Endpoint Protection Solutions project plan execution?

814. What type of information goes in the quality assurance plan?

815. What are the critical steps involved in selecting measures and initiatives?

3.1 Team Member Status Report: Endpoint Protection Solutions

816. Are your organizations Endpoint Protection Solutions projects more successful over time?

817. What specific interest groups do you have in place?

818. What is to be done?

819. How can you make it practical?

820. Does your organization have the means (staff, money, contract, etc.) to produce or to acquire the product, good, or service?

821. Is there evidence that staff is taking a more professional approach toward management of your organizations Endpoint Protection Solutions projects?

822. Does every department have to have a Endpoint Protection Solutions project Manager on staff?

823. Why is it to be done?

824. How will resource planning be done?

825. When a teams productivity and success depend on collaboration and the efficient flow of information, what generally fails them?

826. Are the attitudes of staff regarding Endpoint

Protection Solutions project work improving?

827. Does the product, good, or service already exist within your organization?

828. Will the staff do training or is that done by a third party?

829. How it is to be done?

830. Do you have an Enterprise Endpoint Protection Solutions project Management Office (EPMO)?

831. How does this product, good, or service meet the needs of the Endpoint Protection Solutions project and your organization as a whole?

832. How much risk is involved?

833. Are the products of your organizations Endpoint Protection Solutions projects meeting customers objectives?

834. The problem with Reward & Recognition Programs is that the truly deserving people all too often get left out. How can you make it practical?

3.2 Change Request: Endpoint Protection Solutions

835. Who is responsible to authorize changes?

836. What are the duties of the change control team?

837. Who is communicating the change?

838. Who will perform the change?

839. Does the schedule include Endpoint Protection Solutions project management time and change request analysis time?

840. How many times must the change be modified or presented to the change control board before it is approved?

841. How to get changes (code) out in a timely manner?

842. How are the measures for carrying out the change established?

843. How is the change documented (format, content, storage)?

844. Are there requirements attributes that are strongly related to the complexity and size?

845. Will this change conflict with other requirements changes (e.g., lead to conflicting operational

scenarios)?

846. What are the requirements for urgent changes?

847. Are there requirements attributes that can discriminate between high and low reliability?

848. What needs to be communicated?

849. How do you get changes (code) out in a timely manner?

850. Will the change use memory to the extent that other functions will be not have sufficient memory to operate effectively?

851. Is it feasible to use requirements attributes as predictors of reliability?

852. Who is included in the change control team?

853. How is quality being addressed on the Endpoint Protection Solutions project?

3.3 Change Log: Endpoint Protection Solutions

854. How does this change affect the timeline of the schedule?

855. Is the submitted change a new change or a modification of a previously approved change?

856. Is this a mandatory replacement?

857. Is the change backward compatible without limitations?

858. Do the described changes impact on the integrity or security of the system?

859. Should a more thorough impact analysis be conducted?

860. Is the change request within Endpoint Protection Solutions project scope?

861. How does this change affect scope?

862. Will the Endpoint Protection Solutions project fail if the change request is not executed?

863. Is the change request open, closed or pending?

864. Who initiated the change request?

865. When was the request approved?

866. Does the suggested change request represent a desired enhancement to the products functionality?

867. Does the suggested change request seem to represent a necessary enhancement to the product?

868. When was the request submitted?

869. Is the requested change request a result of changes in other Endpoint Protection Solutions project(s)?

870. How does this relate to the standards developed for specific business processes?

3.4 Decision Log: Endpoint Protection Solutions

871. How do you know when you are achieving it?

872. How does provision of information, both in terms of content and presentation, influence acceptance of alternative strategies?

873. Linked to original objective?

874. Decision-making process; how will the team make decisions?

875. What are the cost implications?

876. Adversarial environment. is your opponent open to a non-traditional workflow, or will it likely challenge anything you do?

877. What is the average size of your matters in an applicable measurement?

878. Do strategies and tactics aimed at less than full control reduce the costs of management or simply shift the cost burden?

879. How do you define success?

880. How effective is maintaining the log at facilitating organizational learning?

881. What is your overall strategy for quality control /

quality assurance procedures?

882. What alternatives/risks were considered?

883. Meeting purpose; why does this team meet?

884. It becomes critical to track and periodically revisit both operational effectiveness; Are you noticing all that you need to, and are you interpreting what you see effectively?

885. What eDiscovery problem or issue did your organization set out to fix or make better?

886. Who is the decisionmaker?

887. What is the line where eDiscovery ends and document review begins?

888. At what point in time does loss become unacceptable?

889. What was the rationale for the decision?

890. How does an increasing emphasis on cost containment influence the strategies and tactics used?

3.5 Quality Audit: Endpoint Protection Solutions

891. Are measuring and test equipment that have been placed out of service suitably identified and excluded from use in any device reconditioning operation?

892. What mechanisms exist for identification of staff development needs?

893. How does your organization know that its staff have appropriate access to a fair and effective grievance process?

894. How does your organization know that its system for attending to the particular needs of its international staff is appropriately effective and constructive?

895. Have the risks associated with the intentions been identified, analyzed and appropriate responses developed?

896. How does your organization know that its relationships with other relevant organizations are appropriately effective and constructive?

897. How does your organization know that its promotions system is appropriately effective, constructive and fair?

898. What does an analysis of your organizations staff

profile suggest in terms of its planning, and how is this being addressed?

899. What data about organizational performance is routinely collected and reported?

900. How does your organization know that the support for its staff is appropriately effective and constructive?

901. How does your organization know that its staff entrance standards are appropriately effective and constructive and being implemented consistently?

902. How does your organization know that its staff support services planning and management systems are appropriately effective and constructive?

903. What review processes are in place for your organizations major activities?

904. How does your organization know that it is appropriately effective and constructive in preparing its staff for organizational aspirations?

905. Is progress against the intentions measurable?

906. It is inappropriate to seek information about the Audit Panels preliminary views including questions like why do you ask that?

907. If your organization thinks it is doing something well, can it prove this?

908. How does your organization know that its management system is appropriately effective and

constructive?

909. How does your organization know that the research supervision provided to its staff is appropriately effective and constructive?

910. Is the process of self review, learning and improvement endemic throughout your organization?

3.6 Team Directory: Endpoint Protection Solutions

911. Decisions: what could be done better to improve the quality of the constructed product?

912. Who will report Endpoint Protection Solutions project status to all stakeholders?

913. Why is the work necessary?

914. Process decisions: which organizational elements and which individuals will be assigned management functions?

915. Have you decided when to celebrate the Endpoint Protection Solutions projects completion date?

916. Who are your stakeholders (customers, sponsors, end users, team members)?

917. Who will be the stakeholders on your next Endpoint Protection Solutions project?

918. Who should receive information (all stakeholders)?

919. Where should the information be distributed?

920. Timing: when do the effects of communication take place?

921. Process decisions: how well was task order work performed?

922. Process decisions: do job conditions warrant additional actions to collect job information and document on-site activity?

923. Decisions: is the most suitable form of contract being used?

924. Who will talk to the customer?

925. Where will the product be used and/or delivered or built when appropriate?

926. Is construction on schedule?

927. Who are the Team Members?

928. Does a Endpoint Protection Solutions project team directory list all resources assigned to the Endpoint Protection Solutions project?

3.7 Team Operating Agreement: Endpoint Protection Solutions

929. Did you prepare participants for the next meeting?

930. Did you recap the meeting purpose, time, and expectations?

931. What individual strengths does each team member bring to the group?

932. Does your team need access to all documents and information at all times?

933. What are the current caseload numbers in the unit?

934. Are there the right people on your team?

935. Do you leverage technology engagement tools group chat, polls, screen sharing, etc.?

936. How do you want to be thought of and known within your organization?

937. Are there influences outside the team that may affect performance, and if so, have you identified and addressed them?

938. What types of accommodations will be formulated and put in place for sustaining the team?

939. Is compensation based on team and individual performance?

940. Are there differences in access to communication and collaboration technology based on team member location?

941. Do you ask participants to close laptops and place mobile devices on silent on the table while the meeting is in progress?

942. Do you begin with a question to engage everyone?

943. What went well?

944. Do you call or email participants to ensure understanding, follow-through and commitment to the meeting outcomes?

945. Do you brief absent members after they view meeting notes or listen to a recording?

946. What resources can be provided for the team in terms of equipment, space, time for training, protected time and space for meetings, and travel allowances?

947. To whom do you deliver your services?

3.8 Team Performance Assessment: Endpoint Protection Solutions

948. What are teams?

949. Individual task proficiency and team process behavior: what is important for team functioning?

950. Where to from here?

951. If you have criticized someones work for method variance in your role as reviewer, what was the circumstance?

952. How do you manage human resources?

953. To what degree does the teams purpose contain themes that are particularly meaningful and memorable?

954. What is method variance?

955. Do you promptly inform members about major developments that may affect them?

956. How hard do you try to make a good selection?

957. Which situations call for a more extreme type of adaptiveness in which team members actually re-define roles?

958. To what degree do members understand and articulate the same purpose without relying on

ambiguous abstractions?

959. To what degree can all members engage in open and interactive considerations?

960. To what degree are sub-teams possible or necessary?

961. To what degree does the teams work approach provide opportunity for members to engage in open interaction?

962. Social categorization and intergroup behaviour: Does minimal intergroup discrimination make social identity more positive?

963. What structural changes have you made or are you preparing to make?

964. Delaying market entry: how long is too long?

965. To what degree do the goals specify concrete team work products?

966. To what degree are the relative importance and priority of the goals clear to all team members?

967. When does the medium matter?

3.9 Team Member Performance Assessment: Endpoint Protection Solutions

968. How do you know that all team members are learning?

969. What are the evaluation strategies (e.g., reaction, learning, behavior, results) used. What evaluation results did you have?

970. What kinds of performance factors / elements do you use?

971. To what degree are the skill areas critical to team performance present?

972. Are any validation activities performed?

973. What is collaboration?

974. What are the basic principles and objectives of performance measurement and assessment?

975. Are the draft goals SMART ?

976. How do you currently account for your results in the teams achievement?

977. What are top priorities?

978. How will you identify your Team Leaders?

979. Are the goals SMART ?

980. What are best practices for delivering and developing training evaluations to maximize the benefits of leveraging emerging technologies?

981. How is performance assessment used in making future award decisions including options and extend/compete decisions?

982. What instructional strategies were developed/incorporated (e.g., direct instruction, indirect instruction, experiential learning, independent study, interactive instruction)?

983. Does the rater (supervisor) have the authority or responsibility to tell an employee that the employees performance is unsatisfactory?

984. What stakeholders must be involved In the development and oversight of the performance plan?

985. What is the role of the Reviewer?

3.10 Issue Log: Endpoint Protection Solutions

986. What is the status of the issue?

987. What effort will a change need?

988. What would have to change?

989. Is there an important stakeholder who is actively opposed and will not receive messages?

990. Which team member will work with each stakeholder?

991. Why do you manage human resources?

992. How is this initiative related to other portfolios, programs, or Endpoint Protection Solutions projects?

993. How do you reply to this question; you am new here and managing this major program. How do you suggest you build your network?

994. Are there too many who have an interest in some aspect of your work?

995. What is a Stakeholder?

996. What is the impact on the Business Case?

997. In your work, how much time is spent on stakeholder identification?

998. Why do you manage communications?

999. Who reported the issue?

1000. Are you constantly rushing from meeting to meeting?

4.0 Monitoring and Controlling Process Group: Endpoint Protection Solutions

1001. How well did the chosen processes fit the needs of the Endpoint Protection Solutions project?

1002. Were escalated issues resolved promptly?

1003. What do they need to know about the Endpoint Protection Solutions project?

1004. When will the Endpoint Protection Solutions project be done?

1005. How well did the team follow the chosen processes?

1006. What factors are contributing to progress or delay in the achievement of products and results?

1007. How many potential communications channels exist on the Endpoint Protection Solutions project?

1008. Are the services being delivered?

1009. What departments are involved in its daily operation?

1010. Is there sufficient funding available for this?

1011. How will staff learn how to use the deliverables?

1012. Did you implement the program as designed?

1013. How well did the chosen processes produce the expected results?

1014. Did it work?

1015. How can you make your needs known?

1016. Do clients benefit (change) from the services?

1017. What kinds of things in particular are you looking for data on?

4.1 Project Performance Report: Endpoint Protection Solutions

1018. To what degree does the team possess adequate membership to achieve its ends?

1019. To what degree does the task meet individual needs?

1020. To what degree can the cognitive capacity of individuals accommodate the flow of information?

1021. To what degree will the approach capitalize on and enhance the skills of all team members in a manner that takes into consideration other demands on members of the team?

1022. To what degree do the structures of the formal organization motivate taskrelevant behavior and facilitate task completion?

1023. To what degree is the team cognizant of small wins to be celebrated along the way?

1024. To what degree are the goals ambitious?

1025. To what degree does the information network communicate information relevant to the task?

1026. To what degree does the teams purpose constitute a broader, deeper aspiration than just accomplishing short-term goals?

1027. What degree are the relative importance and priority of the goals clear to all team members?

1028. To what degree does the funding match the requirement?

1029. To what degree does the formal organization make use of individual resources and meet individual needs?

1030. To what degree can the team measure progress against specific goals?

1031. To what degree will each member have the opportunity to advance his or her professional skills in all three of the above categories while contributing to the accomplishment of the teams purpose and goals?

1032. To what degree are the demands of the task compatible with and converge with the relationships of the informal organization?

1033. Next Steps?

1034. To what degree are fresh input and perspectives systematically caught and added (for example, through information and analysis, new members, and senior sponsors)?

1035. To what degree are the members clear on what they are individually responsible for and what they are jointly responsible for?

4.2 Variance Analysis: Endpoint Protection Solutions

1036. Can process improvements lead to unfavorable variances?

1037. Is there a logical explanation for any variance?

1038. At what point should variances be isolated and brought to the attention of the management?

1039. Is cost and schedule performance measurement done in a consistent, systematic manner?

1040. Are all budgets assigned to control accounts?

1041. What business event caused the fluctuation?

1042. Does the accounting system provide a basis for auditing records of direct costs chargeable to the contract?

1043. Is the anticipated (firm and potential) business base Endpoint Protection Solutions projected in a rational, consistent manner?

1044. Are the bases and rates for allocating costs from each indirect pool consistently applied?

1045. How are material, labor, and overhead variances calculated and recorded?

1046. Does the scheduling system identify in a timely

manner the status of work?

1047. What was the cause of the increase in costs?

1048. Are records maintained to show how management reserves are used?

1049. Does the contractor use objective results, design reviews and tests to trace schedule performance?

1050. Is budgeted cost for work performed calculated in a manner consistent with the way work is planned?

1051. What costs are avoidable if one or more customers are dropped?

1052. Are overhead cost budgets established for each department which has authority to incur overhead costs?

1053. Are the overhead pools formally and adequately identified?

1054. Do the rates and prices remain constant throughout the year?

4.3 Earned Value Status: Endpoint Protection Solutions

1055. Earned value can be used in almost any Endpoint Protection Solutions project situation and in almost any Endpoint Protection Solutions project environment. it may be used on large Endpoint Protection Solutions projects, medium sized Endpoint Protection Solutions projects, tiny Endpoint Protection Solutions projects (in cut-down form), complex and simple Endpoint Protection Solutions projects and in any market sector. some people, of course, know all about earned value, they have used it for years - but perhaps not as effectively as they could have?

1056. Validation is a process of ensuring that the developed system will actually achieve the stakeholders desired outcomes; Are you building the right product? What do you validate?

1057. How much is it going to cost by the finish?

1058. Are you hitting your Endpoint Protection Solutions projects targets?

1059. Where is evidence-based earned value in your organization reported?

1060. Verification is a process of ensuring that the developed system satisfies the stakeholders agreements and specifications; Are you building the product right? What do you verify?

1061. What is the unit of forecast value?

1062. If earned value management (EVM) is so good in determining the true status of a Endpoint Protection Solutions project and Endpoint Protection Solutions project its completion, why is it that hardly any one uses it in information systems related Endpoint Protection Solutions projects?

1063. How does this compare with other Endpoint Protection Solutions projects?

1064. When is it going to finish?

1065. Where are your problem areas?

4.4 Risk Audit: Endpoint Protection Solutions

1066. Does the Endpoint Protection Solutions project team have experience with the technology to be implemented?

1067. Estimated size of product in number of programs, files, transactions?

1068. Does your organization have or has considered the need for insurance covers: public liability, professional indemnity and directors and officers liability?

1069. What are the benefits of a Enterprise wide approach to Risk Management?

1070. What are the outcomes you are looking for?

1071. Do you meet the legislative requirements (for example PAYG, super contributions) for paid employees?

1072. What are the risks that could stop you from achieving your objectives?

1073. Tradeoff: how much risk can be tolerated and still deliver the products where they need to be?

1074. Do you ensure the recommended rules of play and protocols are followed for your activity?

1075. Do you record and file all audits?

1076. Who is responsible for what?

1077. How can the strategy fail/achieved?

1078. What events or circumstances could affect the achievement of your objectives?

1079. To what extent are auditors influenced by the business risk assessment in the audit process, and how can auditors create more effective mental models to more fully examine contradictory evidence?

1080. Are enough people available?

1081. Number of users of the product?

1082. Are corresponding safety and risk management policies posted for all to see?

1083. If applicable; which route/packaging option do you choose for transport of hazmat material?

4.5 Contractor Status Report: Endpoint Protection Solutions

1084. How is risk transferred?

1085. Who can list a Endpoint Protection Solutions project as organization experience, your organization or a previous employee of your organization?

1086. What is the average response time for answering a support call?

1087. Are there contractual transfer concerns?

1088. What was the final actual cost?

1089. What are the minimum and optimal bandwidth requirements for the proposed solution?

1090. What process manages the contracts?

1091. Describe how often regular updates are made to the proposed solution. Are corresponding regular updates included in the standard maintenance plan?

1092. If applicable; describe your standard schedule for new software version releases. Are new software version releases included in the standard maintenance plan?

1093. How long have you been using the services?

1094. What was the budget or estimated cost for your

organizations services?

1095. What was the actual budget or estimated cost for your organizations services?

1096. What was the overall budget or estimated cost?

4.6 Formal Acceptance: Endpoint Protection Solutions

1097. What lessons were learned about your Endpoint Protection Solutions project management methodology?

1098. What function(s) does it fill or meet?

1099. How well did the team follow the methodology?

1100. Do you buy-in installation services?

1101. Did the Endpoint Protection Solutions project manager and team act in a professional and ethical manner?

1102. General estimate of the costs and times to complete the Endpoint Protection Solutions project?

1103. Do you perform formal acceptance or burn-in tests?

1104. How does your team plan to obtain formal acceptance on your Endpoint Protection Solutions project?

1105. Does it do what client said it would?

1106. What are the requirements against which to test, Who will execute?

1107. Is formal acceptance of the Endpoint Protection

Solutions project product documented and distributed?

1108. Do you buy pre-configured systems or build your own configuration?

1109. Was the Endpoint Protection Solutions project managed well?

1110. What features, practices, and processes proved to be strengths or weaknesses?

1111. Who would use it?

1112. Have all comments been addressed?

1113. Who supplies data?

1114. Was the Endpoint Protection Solutions project goal achieved?

1115. Was the client satisfied with the Endpoint Protection Solutions project results?

1116. Does it do what Endpoint Protection Solutions project team said it would?

5.0 Closing Process Group: Endpoint Protection Solutions

1117. Were decisions made in a timely manner?

1118. What is an Encumbrance?

1119. How will you know you did it?

1120. Is this a follow-on to a previous Endpoint Protection Solutions project?

1121. What were the desired outcomes?

1122. Did you do things well?

1123. Were cost budgets met?

1124. When will the Endpoint Protection Solutions project be done?

1125. What will you do?

1126. Is there a clear cause and effect between the activity and the lesson learned?

1127. Did you do what you said you were going to do?

1128. How well defined and documented were the Endpoint Protection Solutions project management processes you chose to use?

1129. Were the outcomes different from the already

stated planned?

1130. What business situation is being addressed?

1131. Can the lesson learned be replicated?

1132. What were things that you need to improve?

5.1 Procurement Audit: Endpoint Protection Solutions

1133. Did the chosen procedure ensure fair competition and transparency?

1134. Are prices always included on the purchase order?

1135. Does the individual approving disbursements sign or initial the document?

1136. Has your organization taken a well-grounded decision about the procurement procedure chosen and has it documented the process?

1137. Was a sufficient competitive environment created?

1138. Were results of the award procedures published?

1139. Is there no evidence that the consultants participating in the Endpoint Protection Solutions project design released information to contractors competing for the prime contract?

1140. Does the approval include approval of prices?

1141. Are employees with cash disbursement responsibilities required to take scheduled vacations?

1142. Are the responsibilities of the purchasing

department clearly defined?

1143. Has management taken the necessary steps to ensure that relevant control systems are always up to date?

1144. Do appropriate controls ensure that procurement decisions are not biased by conflicts of interest or corruption?

1145. Is there a form specified for bids?

1146. How do you avoid delays at any stage/ stages of the procurement process?

1147. Has it been determined which areas of procurement the audit should cover?

1148. Is your organization transparent about winning bids and prices?

1149. Has the award included no items different from the already stated contained in bid specifications?

1150. Are blank purchase order forms protected?

1151. Do staff involved in the various stages of the process have the appropriate skills and training to perform duties effectively?

1152. Are information gathered to produce knowledge about procured goods and services, prices paid and supplier performance?

5.2 Contract Close-Out: Endpoint Protection Solutions

1153. Has each contract been audited to verify acceptance and delivery?

1154. Change in circumstances?

1155. Have all acceptance criteria been met prior to final payment to contractors?

1156. Why Outsource?

1157. Was the contract type appropriate?

1158. Was the contract sufficiently clear so as not to result in numerous disputes and misunderstandings?

1159. How/when used ?

1160. How is the contracting office notified of the automatic contract close-out?

1161. What happens to the recipient of services?

1162. Change in attitude or behavior?

1163. Are the signers the authorized officials?

1164. Have all contract records been included in the Endpoint Protection Solutions project archives?

1165. Change in knowledge?

1166. Parties: Authorized?

1167. Was the contract complete without requiring numerous changes and revisions?

1168. Parties: who is involved?

1169. Have all contracts been completed?

1170. What is capture management?

1171. Have all contracts been closed?

1172. How does it work?

5.3 Project or Phase Close-Out: Endpoint Protection Solutions

1173. What benefits or impacts does the stakeholder group expect to obtain as a result of the Endpoint Protection Solutions project?

1174. What stakeholder group needs, expectations, and interests are being met by the Endpoint Protection Solutions project?

1175. What hierarchical authority does the stakeholder have in your organization?

1176. What information is each stakeholder group interested in?

1177. How often did each stakeholder need an update?

1178. What is a Risk?

1179. What are the marketing communication needs for each stakeholder?

1180. Which changes might a stakeholder be required to make as a result of the Endpoint Protection Solutions project?

1181. What is this stakeholder expecting?

1182. Who is responsible for award close-out?

1183. Were risks identified and mitigated?

1184. What are the mandatory communication needs for each stakeholder?

1185. Was the schedule met?

1186. Is the lesson significant, valid, and applicable?

1187. Who exerted influence that has positively affected or negatively impacted the Endpoint Protection Solutions project?

1188. What is a Risk Management Process?

1189. Did the delivered product meet the specified requirements and goals of the Endpoint Protection Solutions project?

1190. In preparing the Lessons Learned report, should it reflect a consensus viewpoint, or should the report reflect the different individual viewpoints?

5.4 Lessons Learned: Endpoint Protection Solutions

1191. How accurately and timely was the Risk Management Log updated or reviewed?

1192. Do you have any real problems?

1193. How well was Endpoint Protection Solutions project status communicated throughout your involvement in the Endpoint Protection Solutions project?

1194. Is your organization willing to expose problems or mistakes for the betterment of the collective whole, and can you do this in a way that does not intimidate employees or workers?

1195. To what extent was the evolution of risks communicated?

1196. What could be done to improve the process?

1197. How effective were Best Practices & Lessons Learned from prior Endpoint Protection Solutions projects utilized in this Endpoint Protection Solutions project?

1198. How many government and contractor personnel are authorized for the Endpoint Protection Solutions project?

1199. What would you approach differently next time?

1200. Was sufficient advance training conducted and/or information provided to enable the already stated affected by the changes to adjust to and accommodate them?

1201. How adequately involved did you feel in Endpoint Protection Solutions project decisions?

1202. How well were Endpoint Protection Solutions project issues communicated throughout your involvement in the Endpoint Protection Solutions project?

1203. For the next Endpoint Protection Solutions project, how could you improve on the way Endpoint Protection Solutions project was conducted?

1204. What other questions should you have asked?

1205. How well does the product or service the Endpoint Protection Solutions project produced meet the defined Endpoint Protection Solutions project requirements?

1206. Did the team work well together?

1207. What are the internal fiscal constraints?

1208. How effectively and consistently was sponsorship for the Endpoint Protection Solutions project conveyed?

1209. What is the frequency of communication?

1210. How effective was the documentation that

you received with the Endpoint Protection Solutions project product/service?

Index

CPSIA information can be obtained
at www.ICGtesting.com
Printed in the USA
BVHW041009200819

556236BV00011B/647/P